The Central Buttress of Scafell

THE CENTRAL BUTTRESS OF SCAFELL

*A collection of essays selected and introduced
by Graham Wilson*

Millrace

First published in Great Britain in 2004 by
Millrace
2a Leafield Road, Disley
Cheshire SK12 2JF
www.millracebooks.co.uk

Introduction and commentary © 2004 Graham Wilson
'An Easy Day for a Lady?' © 2004 Elizabeth Cripps
Illustration on pp 64-5 © 2004 Gerry Dale
Bowline motif © 2004 Jane Droop
Photo on p viii © 2004 Millrace

ISBN: 1 902173 163

Typeset in Berthold Baskerville.
Produced in the United Kingdom
by LPPS Ltd, Wellingborough, Northants NN8 3PJ

Acknowledgements

As the more significant part of what follows consists of articles that have previously appeared in the Journals of the Fell & Rock Climbing Club and the Yorkshire Ramblers' Club, I am more than grateful for permission to reproduce them in their entirety. It would also be appropriate, at this juncture, to acknowledge the work of a succession of Journal editors who have laboured to such effect to maintain a record of the historical development of climbing in the British Isles.

In addition, I would like to thank Jim Perrin, who generously allowed me to quote from his correspondence with Bill Stallybrass. This formed the basis of his research into the first unaided ascent of the Flake by Menlove Edwards, the fruits of which appear in his biography of the climber, *Menlove*, first published by Gollancz in 1985.

The many other sources of information are acknowledged in the footnotes but I would particularly recommend Clark and Pyatt, *Mountaineering in Britain* (1957) and Byne and Sutton, *High Peak* (1966) to anyone interested in the beginnings of the sport.

GPW

In any collection of historic essays, there are inevitably some variations in spelling. We have kept the authors' own renderings of place names, be they Scawfell or Scafell, Wasdale or Wastdale...

The drawing on p 115 is by C D Frankland and accompanied his 1922 article in the Yorkshire Ramblers' Club Journal.

Contents

Central Buttress in snow

Introduction

It can be assumed that when an object is so immediately identifiable by its initials that, as with the BBC, no one bothers to elasticise them, then the object in question has a permanent place in the order of things. To the climbing world in Britain, the combination of the letters C and B can have only one meaning. The ascent of the central buttress of the main rock face of Scafell captured – and continues to capture – the imagination of all those interested, not only in the history of the sport but also in how the breaking of psychological barriers moves the apparently impossible to within the reach of the merely mortal.

But what was it that set apart the challenge of Central Buttress from the other hard climbs in the district? What boundary had it passed to justify the description in the first Fell & Rock climbing guide of 1924 that 'the difficulties met with are so great that the expedition ranks amongst the world's hardest, and is possible only under practically perfect conditions'? Three elements contributed to its singular reputation: the mountain, the crag and the man. And each played a significant part.

Foremost is the mountain itself. Scafell's reputation went before it. Until accurate surveying caught up, it was believed to be the highest hill in England and, indeed, from most viewpoints it looks higher than its satellite Pike. Its renown was further embroidered by Coleridge's account of his traverse of the Fell, which included writing a letter to Sara Hutchinson on the summit and the first recorded rock-climbing descent of Broad Stand.* And, whereas the summit of most mountains in England can be reached from whatever angle the walker chooses, Scafell is an exception. All the popular approaches from the surrounding valleys land you on Mickledore — Coleridge's elegant 'hyphen' between fell and pike — where the way is barred by a series of vertical rocky steps flanked by seemingly impassable buttresses. There is no alternative for the walker but to drop down to the foot of Lord's Rake and slink around the back of the crag to the top. Though the rocky steps of Broad Stand

* For a detailed and scholarly account of the event, see A P Rossiter's letter published in Vol XVI of the FRCC Journal.

should offer little problem to the experienced rock climber and are the quickest way down from most of the routes in the vicinity, the rest of the crag is not so accommodating. A band of buttresses and slabs riven by steep gullies or ghylls protect the north face and until 1931, when Kirkus put up Mickledore Grooves, the unsurmountable rampart around the eastern extremity was not even a consideration. In addition, as these crags lie around the 3,000 foot contour in the wettest part of England, the rock is usually damp and greasy.

In the second half of the nineteenth century, the Victorians chipped away (in Collie's case, all too literally) at the north face. First climbing the gullies and chimneys, then breaking out on to the easier faces, they covered the obvious ground. By the turn of the century, most of the cliff had been explored, with the notable exception of the great central buttress which was bounded by Moss Ghyll to the west and a bracketing shot by the Abraham brothers to the east (Keswick Brothers' Climb, 1897). At this point, exploration virtually stopped. Between 1904 and 1911 there was only one new climb, Woodhead's, on the whole crag, as opposed to six on Pillar, thirteen in Langdale and fourteen on Dow, and it was thought that any further exploration was, if not impossible, certainly unjustifiable – the limit had been reached and the greater challenge of a sullen block of rock 200 feet wide and 400 feet high was left to its own devices.

There was a variety of reasons for this. Paramount among these was the accident in 1903, where four men were killed whilst attempting to force a direct route from Lord's Rake to Hopkinson's cairn. It provided the platform that the mountaineering establishment had been waiting for. The Alpine Club thundered over reckless groups of young men racing against each other for the notoriety of first ascents, the absence of professional guides and the formation of modern climbing clubs that stimulated but never restrained. These *obiter dicta* must have had an effect on the ambitions of the climbing fraternity at Wasdale and may indeed have delayed the formation of the Fell & Rock Climbing Club itself.

In addition, most of the taxing climbs on the crag had been pioneered by O G Jones and there was good reason to see him and his routes as the sort of phenomenon that appears maybe once in a generation. Not only was he exceptionally strong (he once raised his chin three times above a horizontal bar using three fingers of his left hand, while simultaneously lifting a fully grown man off the ground with his right, and, on another occasion, girdled a steam-engine using only the rivet heads for foot- and handholds)* but he was also regarded by his contemporaries as the best 'cragsman' they had ever encountered. He, in addition, applied an engineer's mind to the construction of belays and human pyramids which, though precarious, were mechanically safe. A combination of these attributes allowed the parties he led to produce a series of 'exceptionally severe' courses on the crags around Wasdale. His death in the Alps when involved in similar combined tactics (though ironically as the prop to the obligatory guide whose fall caused the disaster) must have reinforced the case that the new harder routes on Scafell were beyond the ambit of the normal man and any further attempts on the open faces were not only unjustified but irresponsible.

And there was always the location. Often 'out of condition', it must have been tempting to look elsewhere. It is interesting to speculate whether a route as difficult as Eagle's Nest Direct would have been contemplated in 1892 if it had been perched half-way

* *Mountain Adventures at Home and Abroad*, G D Abraham, 1910.

up Scafell instead of the south-facing Napes. Climbers found cliffs and hotels in sunnier, or at least drier, climes and the hegemony of Wasdale began to falter. In fact, it was a group based around the Coniston area that was most instrumental in founding the Fell & Rock Climbing Club. A journal followed immediately and its first edition led with an article by the President, which addressed the situation as he saw it and bewailed the lack of ambition of the current members.

As for the man, Siegfried Wedgwood Herford had yet to arrive.

An Hour in the Smoke Room at Wastdale

Ashley P Abraham, 1907

Upon a certain Good Friday night, considerably less than a hundred years ago, the little smoke room at Wastdale was filled almost to overflowing with those peculiar people who most frequent it at that period of the year.

The greater part of them smoked and talked incessantly. Some few occupied chairs, while others perched insecurely on the edges of various articles of furniture, the while mechanically preserving their balance by some of the unusual methods they had resorted to on the rocks during the day. Others, and they were in a majority, descended to more primitive habits, and occupied most of the available floor space.

The atmosphere was laden with tobacco smoke. It was almost as difficult to see across the room as it is to catch a sight of Collier's Climb from Mickledore Ridge on a cloudy day. And to make oneself heard across the chatter of conversation was quite as impossible as it is in a high wind to hear the summons to 'come on' from one's leader at the top of

Slingsby's Chimney on Scawfell Pinnacle, when one is shivering on the small, well-worn ledge above the 'crevasse'.

The occupants of the room formed a motley crowd. Probably nowhere save at a climbing centre could such a gathering be found. Their garb for the most part was quite unusual, and ranged in detail from the latest fashionable evening dress to a certain torn and tattered brown Norfolk jacket, the only respectable part of which was the silken chamois-portraying badge of the Swiss Alpine Club. The coat was a relic of the late Owen Jones, and its present wearer looked upon it as his especial evening property when staying at the inn. Its juxtaposition to the 'proper' garments of the present day afforded, to those who were in a position to observe it, an indication of the change that has come over the habitués of Wastdale; and its wearer, an 'Old Stager' whose knowledge of the surrounding rocks dated back more than twenty years, formed almost as great a contrast to most of those about him as did his apparel to theirs. He was seated on the floor at the corner of the hearth-stone, and was for a time one of the few silent men in the place. After a while he got up, and going to the window threw it wide open, somewhat to the disgust of many of his companions. But before long he was to raise an even greater dissent amongst them, and tread pretty effectually on one of their most cherished tenets.

The lull in the conversation which followed the admission of the fresh air was broken by two men sitting in the armchair at the side of the room most removed from the fire.

'What do you think of Moss Ghyll for to-morrow?' asked the one of the other.

'Oh! Moss Ghyll's all right, but it doesn't fill in a day you know. Ten years ago men used to waste a whole day on it, and return to Wastdale in the evening, jolly well pleased with themselves. But just a week ago we went up Scawfell Pinnacle from the Second Pitch in Deep Ghyll, and then down Professor's Chimney and up the Great Chimney opposite. Even then it was too soon to come home, so we rattled down the Penrith climb and then climbed Moss Ghyll by Collier's exit, coming down to Mickledore again by way of the two pitches in Deep Ghyll.'

Silence greeted this confession. There was an atmosphere of something amiss when such a number of standard courses could be crowded into one day's climbing.

The Old Stager on the corner of the hearth-stone proceeded to lay his finger most unpleasantly on the cause.

'More's the pity!' growled he.

'Why?' queried he of the many ascents.

'Well, perhaps you may not be altogether pleased if I tell you. However, has it never struck you that when a small matter of ten years works such a change in the amount of climbing possible in one day, there must either be something wrong with the climbs themselves, or else that you present-day climbers are vastly superior to those of ten or twenty years ago?'

'Well, I hadn't thought much about it,' confessed the other, 'but I very much doubt if we present rock climbers are better than some of those of the past.'

'Better?' queried the Old Stager scornfully; 'Do you think you are nearly as good?' – 'Pardon my seeming rudeness,' he hastened to say. 'It has not been my privilege to climb with you; but, again pardon my speaking plainly, it must be apparent by your achievements that you cannot be quite as good. However good you may be in the actual climbing, it seems to me that you lack initiative. Where are the new climbs of the present day? What have you to set against Moss Ghyll, Scawfell Pinnacle Arête,

North Climb on the Pillar, the Napes Arêtes, and so on, to mention a few of the good standard climbs? And what have you in the way of difficult climbs to beat Eagle's Nest Arête, Walker's Gully, the C Gully on the Screes, or Jones' Climb up Scawfell Pinnacle from Lord's Rake?'

'Oh, surely!' exclaimed many in the room, all anxious to speak at once.

But the Old Stager had spoken to the man of many ascents, and looked to him for an answer. The field opened up by the other's queries was such a wide one that he found some difficulty in selecting the most effective reply.

After a moment's pause, however, he began.

'Well, I think you lose sight of a certain truism. You forget that now these things have been climbed we cannot make the first ascent of them! I don't for a moment wish to institute a comparison of ourselves with those illustrious men who climbed the things you have just mentioned. I fear we should emerge feeling very ridiculous. But I think you must do us the justice of admitting that there are no new climbs round here but what would prove exceptionally severe, and I know you would condemn these. It's like your "old school" to come down on us like "a

thousand of bricks" if we climb anything very difficult. You lose sight of those difficult things you were
gloating over just now! You forget that Jones' ascent
of Walker's Gully, and Collier's exploit on his Scawfell Climb, and Haskett-Smith's solitary ascent of
the Needle, or, even more daring still, G A Solly's
leading up the Eagle's Nest Arête don't leave much
room for your school to preach caution and wisdom!
But I'm getting a bit off the route. What we really
lack is the possibility of new ascents. They are all
exhausted, and I think you must admit as much!'

'Not at all,' immediately returned the Old Stager.
'There are any amount of new things just itching to
be climbed! I can think of at least a dozen, and if you
don't hurry up and do them, instead of making more
evident the routes up the standard climbs, you'll
have some of the older men returning and robbing
you of them.'

'Where are these new climbs?' cried the others.
'Tell us one!'

'Ah, no! to tell you of them would be foolish on
my part. You would climb them and begin to fancy
yourselves; then that modesty, which all must admit
is one of your strongest qualities, would be likely to
vanish.'

All this with a twinkle in the speaker's eye and certain evidences of discomfort on the part of the others. They feared they were being 'got at.'

'But I think I must change my mind about giving away new climbs, and ask you a question. Have any of you ever noticed a bayonet-shaped crack descending from the skyline about midway between Moss Ghyll and Botterill's Crack on Scawfell? No? Has it never occurred to you that between these two climbs there is a stretch of nearly two hundred feet of unscaled rock? No? I bear in mind Collier's and Keswick Brothers' Climbs which follow such a bayonet-shaped line, and rather fancy this third course – but you must just take my suggestion for what it is worth.'

Distrustful, furtive glances exchanged between the leaders of the various parties in the room, spoke of a certain hasty resolve. It materialised early next morning when three strong parties raced up to the 'bayonet-shaped crack.' After spending four futile hours thereabouts, they hastened down to Wastdale, intent upon slaying the Old Stager. He had retreated via Drigg, however, so let us return to the previous night in the smoke room.

'But I also have digressed,' resumed the Old Stager. 'I said "more's the pity" when you told me of your day's climbing on Scawfell, and you wondered why. Well, I'll tell you, though I know that at first you'll probably disagree with me. The reason of your being able to accomplish in one day more than was possible in bygone days, is that the Wastdale climbs have, almost without exception, become easier.'

'Rubbish!' 'Nothing of the sort!' 'Don't you deceive yourself!' 'Quite impossible!' 'They're more difficult!' and other like exclamations were roared from all parts of the room.

But when the storm had abated somewhat the Old Stager was still smiling serenely. To obtain silence, he waved in the air the black companion of many climbs, and his bearing was that of a man who is confident of his ability to make good his position.

'Now,' said he, 'let us discuss this matter quietly. To many of you my remark must sound like rank sacrilege. The word easy is not wont to be connected with the climbing around Wastdale, and, indeed, there can surely be no more difficult climbing any-where. Here the best rock climbers in the kingdom have foregathered. In the pink of training and often fresh from a curtailed Swiss holiday, they have climbed things that are just about as difficult as are humanly possible. My remarks are intended chiefly to apply to a few of the standard courses which I am in a position to speak of as they were soon after they were first climbed, and to contrast their difficulty then with what it is now.'

The company gathered closer round him and waited with evident impatience while their mentor lighted his pipe.

'Now let us take Moss Ghyll since it was a reference to it that started this discussion. When I first climbed Moss Ghyll it had already been climbed some half-dozen times, and still it was much more difficult than now. The holds on the rock face leading to Tennis Court Ledge were much scarcer than they are at present, and the traverse back into the Ghyll was coated with moss. The Collie step was then unmistakable but nowadays the slab on which it occurs contains so many good footholds that even Dr Collie himself would be puzzled to tell you which is his original step. As for the Chimney near the top of the Ghyll, the "through route" has become so enlarged that almost anyone can get through inside, and so obviate that awkward traverse back to the "sentry box". And then again, the Pinnacle from Steep Ghyll: it used to be considered quite impossible to get into Slingsby's Chimney without the aid of a shoulder. Aye! even as recently as seven years ago. But nowadays nobody dares to ask for such a thing. Why? Because doubtful holds have been cleared away, leaving firm spikes of rock underneath. Footholds have been disclosed or accidentally enlarged. With every ascent it seems to have become simpler. Collier's Climb also is a place that has undergone a great change. You will no doubt remember the fact that Owen Jones found a shoulder insufficient, but needed the extra inches that his companion's head afforded; and yet I sat to-day on Mickledore Ridge and watched the leaders of two different parties climb that initial thirty feet without even so much as a push from behind. They evidently found the bulge difficult to round, but they did it. Prompted by curiosity I went along the Progress and had a look at the lower part, and was not surprised to find that a great mass of rock has come out of the corner. This has left small holds which can be relied on till a height is reached where it is quite possible to step upward to the right on to the overhanging part.'

The comparisons of the Old Stager were followed eagerly and were generally, although somewhat reluctantly, approved. It had often seemed that some of the climbs bore a reputation for difficulty which was more or less undeserved, and they had been at a loss to account for the discrepancy.

'And what about the Gable climbs? Have they become easier? Surely the Needle, at all events, has become more difficult?' queried a man who that day had, after great effort, managed to climb it.

'Ah, yes,' acquiesced the other, 'I really think the Needle is more difficult than it was. That step up to the left from the horizontal crack below the top boulder is more difficult to take. It has got worn very smooth and rounded. A well-known expert once jocularly threatened to knock that hold away, and so make the Needle impossible. His threat is being slowly fulfilled by those who timidly scratch their boot nails along it to see if it is sufficient to support their weight. It is still quite a good foothold, however. Only yesterday I was sitting in the "dress circle" and saw the leader of a party lose his hold on the top and slither down the boulder, until, most luckily, his toe caught the hold and didn't slip off. That was a narrow shave and a most unpleasant sight. I hear a rumour that the top boulder is loose, but I don't think it can be or it would have come off then. But the Needle must be treated with great respect; in any case, with a good deal more than it gets, or it will retaliate very roughly before long. Just think of it, there were three men on the top at once to-day, all leading different parties, and they spun a coin to determine which should "clear out" and allow the others to come up. It would have been vastly amusing had it not been so fraught with danger. Most of the other Gable climbs that I have visited lately strike me as having become easier, but of this I can only speak personally; in other words I have been able during this visit to lead up climbs with more ease than I did in the old days. And this in spite of increasing years and stiffening joints! I was much shocked to find an artificial step on Kern Knotts. That is a bad sign. I hear it has been there for some time, however, so perhaps its author has decided to "rest on his oars". He ought certainly to be made to lead up the crack!' This idea met with the hearty approval of all. Then the Old Stager resumed, 'I am not sure, on second thoughts, that such a punishment would fit his crime, for the crack also has become very much easier. It was my good fortune to be concerned in one of the earliest ascents, and I am astonished to find the number of good holds now that certainly did not exist then. But perhaps it is just as well. It is the sort of place that needed to become easier, and, in all conscience, it is still difficult enough.'

'What about the Eagle's Nest Arête?' queried a man from the other side of the fireplace.

'Oh, I only climbed that for the first time last week, and it really was very bad. I wouldn't lead up that for the proverbial "thousand pounds". All I can say is, that if it has got easier, the men who first climbed it must have had their triumph tempered with thankfulness when they emerged safely at the top of the first eighty feet. And then there's the Pillar. I hear that it is quite a common thing to lead over the Nose. I always had an idea that this was possible for a tall man, however, and this part is probably not any less difficult than formerly. Tall men who know where the handhold round the corner is, may now lead up it safely. The glamour of difficulty has been dispelled by an increased knowledge of the place. No doubt many other climbs have become easier for this reason, but in many cases, besides those I have mentioned, their easier ascent is due to structural alterations, chiefly brought about by people climbing them. There are two other reasons that occur to me. One is that nearly all loose rock has been removed – there is now hardly any need to test the holds, and the other is that the footholds can be found at once, because of the boot-nail scratches. These things mean not only easier climbing, but also that the climbs can be done with less delay and testing of holds than formerly. And now I trust you will consider I have made good my assertion, and given the reason why our friend here had such a huge "bag" last week. I would just like to add that, although many of the Wastdale climbs have fallen from their once proud vantage of difficulty, they are still, in most cases, far from being easy. It is, I think, a good thing they have not become more difficult. As they are they demand all one's care, and no one can afford to hold them cheaply. And they provide sport that, as far as the length of the climbs will admit, cannot, I feel sure, be bettered anywhere.'

'Hear! hear!' came from all parts of the room as the party began to break up.

'And now for the one ascent that never becomes easier – the climb upstairs to bed. We used to retire about midnight, but now it is only with a struggle we can manage it at two o'clock. Good-night, gentle-men! Good-night! and, by the way, don't forget the bayonet-shaped crack on Scawfell!'

The article was, in fact, a neatly constructed debate on the state and future of the climbing in the district. The author, Ashley Abraham, was well placed to comment on the situation. Alongside his brother, he had climbed with the pioneers and photographed their routes. There is no doubt that in the course of this he must have examined the possibilities of new lines, both while perched patiently behind the tripod and when studying the proofs. The provocative reference to the 'bayonet-shaped crack' would suggest that there may well have been some previous consideration of a route on the blank face between the climb which he and brother George completed and the bounding cleft of Moss Ghyll.

He also saw that climbing was changing from a challenge into a recreation. Like that other social gathering, golf, groups of three or four men would cover a suitably handicapped course of a length appropriate to the party. The strong would assist the weak and the position of the bunkers was well known. After a period of exercise in the open air, they would retire to the Smoke Room to exchange yarns and tobacco with their fellow enthusiasts.

But what caused this complacency? There must have been a number of influences, but two stand out. One revolved around the nature of the routes they had inherited. The Victorians, for a number of reasons, had favoured gullies of various widths as their lines of attack. (Of the sixty climbs in the whole district climbed before 1903, thirty-five fell into this category; of the twenty-five completed between 1903 and 1914, only seven fell into a similar class.) The choice made sense. If you were describing to the said fellow enthusiast the lie of the land, it was easier to identify the start and progress of a gully than a line on an amorphous slab. In addition, the steps and risers allowed the climb to fall into natural sections or pitches which provided a useful series of platforms to field a falling leader or, if the matter proved too arduous, a choice of bivouac site until the rescue party arrived.

As the difficulties of these courses involved wrestling with bulges or other protuberances and making vertical progress by exerting upward pressure stabilised by friction, the emphasis was on muscular heaving rather than holdless balance. As a bonus, the gullies were likely to hold snow, and so provide proper preparation for the greater challenges to be faced in the Alps. It might also have been the case that, given the fissured nature of the surrounding rock, the obligatory ice-axe jammed in a convenient crack might have been a useful piece of gear to provide the odd hand- or foothold

The other significant factor was the appearance in 1900 of O G Jones' guide, *Rock Climbing in the English Lake District.* Although not the first such handbook (Haskett Smith's *Climbing in the British Isles,* 1894, has that distinction) it differed from its predecessor by attempting to list the climbs in an ascending order of difficulty, so that novices might work their way up the ladder until they reached their ceiling. He also divided the climbs into four classes: Easy, Moderate, Difficult and Exceptionally Severe. The Easy courses were little more than a scramble where progress could be conveniently maintained by the use of the hands as well as the feet; the Moderate were generally a series of irregularly-runged step-ladders, usually separated by commodious ledges.

It was only when a route was classified as Difficult that it could be said that rock climbing as we know it today really began. But we would be wrong to assume that Jones' Difficult courses correspond to present classification. There are varying degrees of difficulty within the range, which would include by current classification Diffs, V Diffs, Severes and even, in one instance, a VS. What the climbs had in common was not similar technical difficulty but that they were all relatively safe and suitable for a party of varying ability. The leader could, if necessary, assist the less able and, if he were to fall, he in turn could probably be held.

The fourth class was a different proposition. As the descriptive hyperbole suggests, there was a yawning gap between Difficult and Exceptionally Severe. Even Jones himself advises that these routes 'are best left alone' and reminds his readers of the Establishment message that

> *The novice must on no account attempt them. He may console himself with the reflection that most of these fancy bits of rock-work are not mountaineering proper, and by remembering that those who first explored these routes, or rather* created *them* [my emphasis] *were not only brilliant gymnasts but experienced and capable cragsmen.**

In reality, if the leader were to fall, the rest of the party would probably be pulled off their holds, as happened with the accident in 1903.

* *Rock Climbing in the English Lake District,* O G Jones, 1900.

If the future of climbing was locked into a mind-set that the only new routes to be attempted were those that naturally existed and that any attempt on steep, exposed rock faces was improper, then there is no doubt that the Old Stager's sparring partner was right in saying that the options had been exhausted. But the audience probably suspected that they were being 'got at' and knew that there might be a case that they were not so much prudent as 'frit'.

Nevertheless, the Old Stager was wrong on one point. There was a climb to set against the heroic achievements of the past. In June 1903, Fred Botterill had successfully completed his eponymous Slab. The Old Stager refers to it as Botterill's Crack but the route, in fact, scorned the security of a comforting crevice and sought instead a long and exposed run-out on the very edge of the rock face.

A New Climb on Scafell Crags

Fred Botterill, 1903

The next day, Wednesday, June 3rd, we arranged to spend another day on the Crags in order to examine the crack to the right of the new climb, and see if a way could be found connecting it with the finish of Keswick Brothers' Climb. Business called the gymnast away, and he left us to proceed to Boot, via Burnmoor, thence to be whirled away into civilisation. During the whole of our visit we had had perfect weather, and that day was no exception. We slowly made our way up Brown Tongue, and leaving our rucksack at the foot of Deep Ghyll walked along the Rake's Progress, taking with us a light axe, which judging by the previous day's experience we were sure would be useful.

At the foot of the climb we roped up and noticed that the time was 12.15 pm. The going, over grass ledges, was found fairly easy, until we reached the narrow crack which may be seen from the Progress. The bottom of this was entirely hidden by grass and earth, which when vigorously attacked with the pick, was dislodged in such quantities as to seriously alarm a party coming over Hollow Stones. The removal of some boulders uncovered a large sloping slab which afforded excellent hand- and footholds and enabled the leader to proceed about fifteen feet up the narrow crack. Clearly no one had been here before, so we made greater efforts to advance; it was absolutely impossible however to do so in the crack, it being only six inches wide and about twelve inches deep, and the sides almost as smooth as the inside of a teacup. The leader reluctantly descended to the aforementioned slab and examined the projecting face of the crack, which leans away towards Scafell Pike at about the same angle as the crack we had ascended the day before. This seemed equally hopeless, the ledges being all inverted and the slabs too smooth to climb with safety. Traversing about twelve feet outwards to the edge formed by one side of the crack and the face of the crags, I saw that with care we could advance some distance up this nose. Clearing away the moss from little cracks here and there I managed to climb slowly upwards for about sixty feet. The holds then dwindled down to little more than finger-end cracks. I looked about me and saw, some twelve feet higher, a little nest about a foot square covered with dried grass. Eight feet higher still was another nest and a traverse leading back to where the crack opened into a respectable chimney. If I could only reach hold of that first nest what remained would be comparatively easy. It seemed to be a more difficult thing than I had ever done but I was anxious to tackle it. Not wishing to part with the axe I seized it between my teeth and with my fingers in the best available cracks I advanced. I cannot tell with certainty how many holds there were; but I distinctly remember that when within two feet of the nest I had a good hold with my right hand on the face, and so ventured with my left to tear away the dried grass on the nest. I also remembered my brother Ramblers, who were at that moment exploring the depths of Gaping Ghyll, and wondered which of us were in the more comfortable situation. However, the grass removed from the ledge, a nice little resting place was exposed – painfully small, but level and quite safe. I scrambled on to it, but on account of the weight of the rope behind me, it was only with great care and some difficulty that I was able to turn round. At last I could sit down on the nest and look around me.

The view was glorious. I could see Scafell Pike

and a party round the cairn. Far below was another group intent on watching our movements, a lady being amongst the party. I once read in a book on etiquette that a gentleman in whatever situation of life should never forget his manners towards the other sex, so I raised my hat, though I wondered if the author had ever dreamed of a situation like mine. I now discovered that our eighty feet of rope had quite run out and that my companions had already attached an additional sixty feet. Further, I began to wonder what had become of my axe, and concluded I must unthinkingly have placed it somewhere lower down. There it was, stuck in a little crack about five feet below me. Not knowing what was yet to come I felt I must recover it, so I lowered myself until I could reach it with my foot. I succeeded in balancing it on my boot, but in bringing it up it slipped and clattering on the rocks for a few feet took a final leap and stuck point downwards in the Rake's Progress. Standing up again I recommenced the ascent and climbed on to the second nest *à cheval,* from where, after a brief rest, I began the traverse back to the crack. This was sensational but perfectly safe. As usual I started with the wrong foot, and after taking two steps was obliged to go back. The next time I started with the left foot, then came the right, again the left, and lastly a long stride with the right brought me into the chimney. The performance was what might have been called a *pas-de-quatre*. Complimentary sounds came from my companions below, but without stopping to acknowledge these I pulled myself up ten feet higher on to a good grass-covered ledge to the right of the crack, smaller but very similar to the Tennis Court Ledge of Moss Ghyll.

'How is it now?' my companions enquired. 'Excellent,' I replied, 'a good belaying pin and just room for three. Do you feel like following?' Without answering me the second man commenced the traverse to the chimney edge whilst I carefully belayed the rope. Up he came in splendid style and without stopping, taking only a quarter the time it had taken me. He then untied and we threw down the 140 feet of rope to our third, who soon joined us. We hailed a climbing friend who was watching from the Progress and invited him to join us, but he very generously refused and said he would hover near lest we might not be able to advance further and so require the aid of a rope from above. We next christened our berth 'Coffin Ledge', built a cairn on it and left our names on a card.

Starting off again, a long stride with the left foot took the leader back into the cracks and a stiff climb of twenty to thirty feet landed us all into an extraordinary chimney, which though only wide enough to comfortably admit the body sideways ran right into the crag for about fifteen feet. Like the crack below it leaned to the left at an angle of seventy degrees or so. About twenty-three feet up, chockstones and debris formed a roof, and suspended in the middle, some six or seven feet below it, were three more chockstones. When the second man had joined me he exclaimed with astonishment: 'What a place! How can we get out?' 'Wait a bit,' I answered, although for the life of me I could not then see a way. However, I went as far as I could into the crack and with restricted use of back and knee climbed upwards until the level of the suspended chockstones was reached; from there a narrow ledge rendered these easily accessible. They were securely wedged and safe to stand upon. The ledge continued along out of the crack until the most outward chockstone of the roof was within reach. This I seized with both hands, and a steady pull upwards landed me into the Puttrell Chimney of Keswick Brothers' Climb.

Our main difficulties now being over, the comparatively easy upper gully was soon finished, and as we clambered out at the top, at 3.45 pm, our climbing friend met us with congratulations on what we all agreed was the hardest three and a half hours' work we had ever done. During the descent we recovered the axe and built a cairn at the foot of the climb.

On our return to the Hotel at night we received cordial congratulations from our friends.

The Yorkshire Ramblers' Club Journal, Vol II, No 5, 1903

The preceding article leaves three questions unanswered. Why (to go back to the President's inaugural address) did the Old Stager not give more credit to Botterill, who, by the time the article was written, had not only completed on sight the hardest climb on Scafell (which had defeated O G Jones) but also, via the North-West Climb, the hardest on Pillar? What was there about Botterill that made him capable of leading routes that would defeat all comers until the arrival of Herford? And, if he really was that good, why did he not do more?

The answer to the first is uncertain. Perhaps the Old Stager did not realise the significance of the climbs. After all, he refers to the Scafell route as a crack and he may not have had first-hand knowledge of the route on Pillar. Again, it is possible that inter-club rivalry was at play. Although Botterill was a member of the Fell & Rock, he and his parties hailed from Leeds and were leading lights in the Yorkshire Ramblers' Club. It would not be the first or, indeed, the last time that the Pennines had separated rival ambitions.

The answer to the second is easier. In addition to

being an outstanding athlete (his brother Arthur was a professional gymnast who on one occasion stood on his head on the top of the Needle*) he was, as a cragsman, simply years ahead of his time. Sansom wrote of him that 'he was a very beautiful climber and could have done as much as Herford, or later Kelly, had he tried.'* By that calculation it would be a quarter of a century before all but the exceptional had caught up with him. To put it in perspective, the measure of the standard he set would be the equivalent of Cenotaph Corner not being regularly repeated until the mid-seventies.

An important reason behind this skill was that he was gritstone-trained. Although outcrop climbing was dismissed as a dangerous irrelevance by a large section of the mountaineering community, there is no doubt about its contribution to the advance of rock climbing in England and Wales. The lack of incut handholds meant that the climber had to rely on the ability to step up in balance, rather than apply the traditional grip'n'pull technique; because the climbs were of no great height, top-roping allowed the individual to test his limits in comparative safety but, most importantly, it suggested a different mind-

* *Mountaineering in Britain*, Clark & Pyatt, 1957.

34

set. Exponents realised that they could gain as much satisfaction from the micro of overcoming the technically difficult as from the macro of conquest. Above all, there must have been a psychological advantage in moving back from gripless holds to the 'jugs' of Wasdale's igneous rock.

Which leads us to the final question of why, with all these advantages, did Botterill achieve so little? Apart from producing the (then) hardest route on Scafell and Pillar, his only contribution was a V Diff on the Napes (Abbey Buttress) and a Moderate on Pavey Ark (Crescent Climb). The straightforward answer, suggested by Sansom's comment, is confirmed in his obituary:

> *My only regret is that he did not undertake more, for I am convinced that he had it in him to display as high capacity in other departments of life as in mountaineering.** *

In simple terms, he was unambitious. (He refused a commission while on active service.) He was a man who did not strive to strive. Indeed, he

> *was almost too kind. Were a weak party in need of a leader, Fred would go [...] out of his way to take them up a course that to him was a simple walk.*

*FRCC Journal, 1920.

Yet there is another comment in his obituary that is even more telling:

> *He was a past master of the art of descent. I am quite sure he never ascended a place he could not descend with absolute safety, and – what is more – that the whole party under his charge could not descend in absolute safety.*

Perhaps what limited his ambition was the lack of a partner as skilful as himself. Someone who was as happy to climb downwards and sideways as he was to climb up. By the time such a man, the author of the following essay, appeared, Fred Botterill, devastated by the death of a climbing partner on Eagle's Nest Direct, had given up climbing.

The Doctrine of Descent

S W Herford, 1914

Perhaps one of the questions most frequently put by one's non-climbing friends concerns climbing down: 'Is it harder than climbing up?' And the curious thing is that they nearly all seem inclined to expect one to answer in the affirmative. They may never in their lives have been near a rock, or even on a steep hillside, but nevertheless have an instinctive feeling that going down must be more difficult. Why is this? It would be rather interesting to know the reason. It probably has some connection with the fact that a slope appears steeper to a man looking down it from the top than to one looking up it from below – an optical illusion which would disappear if the observers were to lean away from the vertical so as to be at right angles to the slope. This most probably has a subconscious influence on most people's thoughts when they ask the question, and also the idea that one is in some way assisting gravity, and ultimately that of falling: these together seem to have a cumulative effect sufficient to form what almost amounts to a conviction where, theoretically, the mind should be perfectly open.

To revert now to the original question, what answer should one give? An unqualified 'Yes' or 'No' will not do, and I hope in the course of this article to make clear, among other things, my own personal views on the matter. I would emphasise the word *personal*; for, while it is possible to make certain comprehensive statements and rules of general application (man being built, for the most part, on the same plan, with two arms at the top and two legs at the bottom, etc), yet, when we consider the less obvious and nicer movements and combinations of movements and attitudes which go to make up style and method, and which determine the degree of effort required for a given person to climb a given piece of rock, then we find that we must differentiate for each individual, for these depend upon his height, build, temperament, and a hundred other factors which among themselves form an infinite number of combinations. This is the reason why it is useless, in describing any pitch, to give exact details of how it is to be climbed.

The subject of 'Climbing Down' can be conveniently taken in three parts: (1) Descending difficult rocks; (2) Descending easy rocks; (3) Roping down excessively difficult or unclimbable rocks. Before considering these separately, it would be as well to keep in mind that in all cases the essential difference between ascending and descending is that in the one case work must be done and energy expended in raising the body upwards against gravity, whilst in the other, muscular effort is only exerted in checking the tendency to fall freely, and, technically, no work is done. This does not mean that, under certain conditions, descending may not be a very tiring proceeding, since the keeping of the muscles in a state of tension will by itself ultimately produce exhaustion. Let us now turn to the first part of the subject, i.e. the descent of difficult rocks. And here we come to a question which is of considerable importance, namely: To what extent are one's movements reversible? Are they, in the descent of a pitch, the same as those used in the ascent, only reckoned backwards? Now it must be pretty obvious to anyone who has had any experience of climbing that there are certain places which people go down in a vastly different manner to that in which they go up. What I have principally in mind are, of course, cracks and chimneys offering no positive holds, and in which friction produced by body-wedging is one's sole support. A supreme instance of this sort of climb is the upper pitch of the well-known Monolith Crack in Wales. True, there are one or two genuine ledges; but these are merely incidents, isolated lapses, in a long drawn-out scheme of caterpillar-like wriggling – arm-wedge, leg-wedge, arm-wedge, leg-wedge, and so on, the monotony being merely broken by an occasional backsliding. Now let us watch a man coming down the place. He may very well have taken ten minutes in getting up; if he knows his business it can be done in not much over ten seconds. There need be no relative motion of the different parts of his body; he can slide down keeping himself quite rigid, merely adjusting his speed by suitable side-pressure. This, of course, applies in general to any similar place; in slightly wider chimneys an effective brake can be obtained by facing outwards and side-pressing with a leg against each wall. If, however, we come to full-size back and foot chimneys the method in its entirety fails; the attitude in this case does not allow of sufficient control over the relative movements of the centres of support on either wall, and a clean drop would quickly result. But even here, although the two points of support cannot well move simultaneously, the back, at any rate, can slide, instead of being pushed clear at each movement as in ascending. However, we can leave it at that; chimneys and cracks are among the less important things in modern rock climbing, at any rate from the point of view of this article. Let us, nevertheless, bear in mind the important modifying effect of friction, which is of general application.

I come now to the free and open climbing of slabs and arêtes, grooves and corners, mantelshelves and noses – in short, the higher forms of the sport. The essence of the whole matter is conveyed in one word – balance. That, of course, is easily said, but what does one really mean by it? It is, in this connection, one of those elusive words to define which is usually to bring on one's head a shower of criticism. I will venture no further than this, that it consists largely in an instinctive anticipation of the effect which a given change of one's attitude will have on the general equilibrium, and in the consequent automatic adjustment of one's movements. This applies more particularly to rapid climbing in which balance acts dynamically in controlling the movements of the limbs, but it is involved in a less perceptible but more subtle manner in the delicate and gradual motions which are required in the ascent of, say, a really hard slab. The question now arises: Is a finer sense of balance required in going down than in going up? In certain instances I think it undoubtedly is. Take, for example, the case of a sloping slab with flat shelving holds on which exact footwork is essential. It is, to start with, much harder to gauge the value of a ledge below one's feet than above it – an important point when the hold slopes. Again, such a hold when tried tentatively with a downward-extended foot has a much worse 'feel' than when the boot is lifted up to it, owing to the fact that the foot tends to meet the rock at an angle instead of lying flat. The combined effect of these two factors is a tendency to get as much support as possible for the hands, with the result that the body is kept close against the rock, even in moderately steep places: this, in turn, merely aggravates the first two causes of difficulty. And this is where balance comes in. Since it implies an instinctive valuation of prospective changes of attitude, it gives confidence, and this is the secret of good footwork, particularly in descending. It enables the sloping holds to be boldly stepped down to, the hands being used to push the body away from, instead of holding it to the rock. The vast difference between the two methods has to be seen to be appreciated; the one, a desperate clinging to insufficient holds, the scraping and scratching of boots, and a general appearance of uncertainty and of impending collapse; the other, a progression of steady downward steps with the body in a graceful and more or less upright position. Now, for all the argument to hold, it is a *sine qua non* that there should be no good handholds. If these are to be found the balance theory can be defied, and this, I am afraid, is what happens in nine cases out of ten. The strain now comes mostly on the arms and the method, besides being ungainly, is of course much more tiring. Modifications in the argument are also necessary if the holds are level, or slope in one's favour, in which case, as a general rule, I find descending easier than ascending. In fact, in some instances, where the holds are far apart, the 'body clear' theory is best discarded, and full use made of friction against the rock. A good example of this sort of slab is that immediately below Hopkinson's Cairn on Scafell Pinnacle. Here the holds consist of level or slightly incut ledges nearly an inch wide, but involving rather long stretches from the one to the other. In descending, the friction of the leg and of the foot as it slides down on to its hold is of considerable assistance, and coming down distinctly easier than going up. This final remark applies, in my opinion, to the hard section of the Eagle's Nest ridge. Here the holds are almost level and of ample size, and, in the upper part at any rate, really fine footwork is nowhere needed: this type of climb, too, offers special opportunities for frictional support in descending. I have already mentioned the slab with sloping holds as being harder to descend than to ascend. The only other case ordinarily met with is, I think, the very steep wall or buttress, and that, of course, with many exceptions. I believe that the difficulty here is almost entirely due to the fact that it is very hard to see where one is putting one's feet; apart from that, I do not think that the steepness has by itself any effect that is not present in the ascent. Those who want to test this statement should descend Kern Knotts West Buttress, which is exceedingly steep for about fifteen feet. I think I have said enough to make clear what I feel to be the general principles involved in the descent of difficult rocks. In matters of such complexity experience must ultimately be our guide and basis of all reasoning, and any theory which attempts to explain actual climbing phenomena must be kept throughout in close touch with the practical side of it to be of any value.

I shall now deal briefly with the second part of the subject: the proper descent of comparatively easy rocks at a moderate angle. Perhaps some readers will think that this is hardly worth any consideration at all: if so, then I feel pretty certain that they must themselves be sadly lacking in experience of what rapid descent (under full control) really means (and that is the only manner of descent on easy rocks worth mentioning). And the fact is that the majority of English-trained climbers are under these conditions painfully slow. The reason for this is not far to seek. The exceptionally high standard of English rock climbing develops a style of its own; a style, it is true, remarkable for its exactness, soundness and general deliberation, but which, if applied to this comparatively easy downhill work, is singularly ineffective. To start with, the 'face-out' method is much too seldom adopted; then, too little use is made of gravity and friction; the whole progression from one hold to the next is too calculated and exact, and each individual hold, instead of being regarded as a mere incident in one continuous passage, too often appears to mark, as it were, the end of one section and the beginning of another. The only remedy for this, as for all other faults, is practice, and if only English climbers would spend more time in descending climbs like the Napes ridges or, better still, the Tryfaen buttresses, and that at the maximum speed consistent with safety, they would go far to remove what is, perhaps, the chief defect of their climbing equipment.

The question of 'roping-down' now remains to be dealt with. This stands in a different category to the preceding forms of descent that I have considered, and little is heard of it in England. I can call to mind only one climb – the Traverse of Scafell – where it is absolutely necessary, but there are many places where it would be highly advisable, and it is not difficult to imagine circumstances in which acquaintance with the best accepted methods would prove of great service. The chief requirements are, in order of importance: *(a)* The rope must be attached so that there is no chance of slipping; *(b)* There must be no risk of collapse through fatigue whilst descending; *(c)* Matters should be so arranged that the rope can be drawn in after the last man is down. The leaving behind of a fixed rope does not redound to the credit of a party, though under certain exceptional circumstances there may be no alternative. The first proceeding in roping down is, of course, to find some spike, bollard, chockstone or projecting mass of rock. There may be some difficulty here, but it is surprising what unsatisfactory looking knobs and protrusions can be used; I have, indeed, seen a guide use a flat triangular corner like that of a table, but this was perhaps going a little too far. The next point to be determined is whether the rope will 'move' when the last man is down. In some cases it may be rather hard to say beforehand, owing to the different lie of the rope and increased friction when pulled from below. If there is any doubt, a loop of spare rope should be used, and the rope for doubling hung on this. The loop, of course, is abandoned. For this purpose, a length of thin alpine line is extremely useful, and saves one the sorrow of cutting up a standard-size rope; it is, incidentally, also often handy in belay work. The manner in which the actual descent is to be made depends largely on circumstances. If it is necessary to rope down steep, holdless rocks for a considerable distance, or if the rope is icy, or the fingers numb or tired, then some method of braking must be adopted. The most complete brake, but one which need only be used in extreme circumstances, is obtained as follows: the doubled rope coming down from the belay is passed under the thigh (the left, say, to fix things) from inside to outside; then in front of and across the body to the right shoulder; across the back and again to the front between the left arm and body; finally, passed over the left fore-arm. This gives such an effective break that there is no downward motion at all unless the sliding of the rope round the body is assisted; this can be done conveniently by the left arm, while the right holds on to the rope from above. As can be imagined descent by this method is slow and laborious, and for ordinary cases where, nevertheless, some sort of brake is required, the arrangement generally used is to pass the rope under the thigh (the left again, say) from inside to outside, and over the left forearm, from which it hangs freely. This allows one to slide down fairly rapidly and with much more comfort than the first method. Lastly, there is no case where no brake at all is used, and reliance placed completely on the hands. The feet can now make adequate use of such holds as there are, particularly if one leans well out, and for short, vertical stretches, or long ones if the angle be moderate this is certainly the most effective way at all. The only difficulty that is likely to occur is in the case when the line of descent is not directly downwards from the belay; considerable skill in the use of the feet is then required to prevent the rope from swinging one off to the side. Another way of roping down for the last man, which differs in principle from the foregoing, is that in which he ties to himself one end of the doubled rope (which runs through a fixed loop) while his companions hold on to the other end, and thus lower him down. This method, of course, causes considerable wear of the loop. It is scarcely necessary, I think, to go into any further details concerning roping down; common-sense will supply anything that is lacking, as indeed it does most of that which has been said. I might, however, mention that most people are rather nervous at their first attempt at roping down an exposed place, and that a little previous practice is usually required to give confidence. The various linking methods can be tried very conveniently from the bough of a tree or down the side of a house.

FRCC Journal, Vol III, No 2, 1914

What Botterill had demonstrated in practice, Herford was now examining in theory. Although 'The Doctrine of Descent' was published after his successful attempt on Scafell, there is little doubt that the article was a resumé of his approach, rather than a blueprint for future action. Like Botterill, Herford had honed his technique on gritstone, especially at Castle Naze, and with Laycock, author of *Some Gritstone Climbs*, climbed up and down most of the available rock in the area.

It would have been this experience that made him realise that the secret of descending steep and relatively holdless rock was with 'the hands being used to push the body away from, instead of holding it to the rock', that is, to remain in balance rather than lowering the body by the arms in the hope that the feet will eventually find some suitable purchase. As with O G Jones before him, Herford brought his engineer's mind to the problem, but combined it with Botterill's grace of movement. The result was an advance in technique that brought even a face as steep and formidable as the central buttress of Scafell within the limits of feasible exploration.

Standing at its foot, even on a dry and windless

day, the buttress must have appeared unassailable, but if the front door is locked, it is always worthwhile to examine the possibility of finding an open window to effect an entry. In climbing terms, this means the girdle traverse. Herford had pioneered such a route on Castle Naze, as had Thomson and Reynolds on Lliwedd. In both these cases, the reason for the change of direction was that 'the field for exploration vertically [had become] exhausted'. But this was certainly not true of the Scafell Girdle. From its exit from Moss Ghyll to its arrival at Botterill's Slab, a series of five pitches totalling nearly 200 feet, it crossed a substantial face of rock which, in the course of the century, was to offer a variety of routes and variations ranging from the Severe of Moss Ghyll Grooves to the E4 of Foxshooter. The greatest of which, of course, was CB itself.

So the Girdle Traverse of Scafell, although a fine expedition in its own right, was to become the transom that opened the possibility of a direct vertical ascent which must have been the pioneers' ultimate ambition. The other pioneer in question was George Sansom. Although Herford gets the credit for leading their clutch of first ascents, I am sure he would have been the first to acknowledge his partner's contribution. Sansom must have been virtually Herford's equal in climbing skill to allow the latter to tackle climbs where the leader was in no position to safeguard his second in the event of a fall. Indeed, it could be argued that the section of the Flake that Sansom led was as difficult and dangerous as the more renowned final fifteen feet.

There may have been one area where he was Herford's superior. He probably had a better eye for a route. This is borne out by an occurrence that followed the completion of the Girdle Traverse. H B Gibson was writing up the account in the Wasdale Climbing Book and put Herford's name first. Herford was against this and said, 'Sansom planned the whole thing, he ought to come first.' Sansom, naturally, supported Gibson, claiming that, as Herford was the bolder climber, he was essentially the leader in this and any other enterprise.*

* *Climbing in Wasdale before the First World War*, G Sansom, 1982.

The Traverse of Scafell Crags

S W Herford, 1912

The idea of making a Girdle Traverse across the face of one of the well-known crags, though perhaps new to Cumberland, cannot claim the merit of complete novelty. Lliwedd was the first to be treated in such a manner. Scafell has now followed, a notable second. That this should be so is a sure sign that the field for exploration vertically is becoming exhausted, and that the energies of climbers seeking after that which is new are being diverted into a new plane – the horizontal. And this mode of progression is not without its special advantages. One has the novel feeling of working in a new dimension, and of seeing the rocks from a different point of view. Then there is ample scope for route-finding, and the climber has perforce to acquire the neglected art, essential to the explorer, of descending difficult rocks, and of using a doubled rope down impossible places. Again, every member of the party has often an equal share of the responsibility, while the delights of leading are divided between the first and last man. I feel, therefore, that I need offer no apology for the description which follows.

On the face of it, Scafell seems scarcely a suitable place for a Traverse. The great unclimbed Central Buttress appears to block the way effectually, and there are several other serious obstacles. I was all the more pleased, therefore, when Sansom wrote to me early in September, suggesting a feasible route right across the crags from Professor's Chimney to the Penrith Climb. An expedition to Wasdale was planned forthwith. On arriving there we were lucky to find both Gibson and Brunskill ready to join us, and the morrow saw all four of us trudging up Brown Tongue with high hopes of completing the expedition that day; but, as it turned out, the hour was rather late for the lengthy job in hand.

Our starting point was the top of the first pitch of Professor's Chimney, and from there we followed Thompson's route to the top of the second pitch of Woodhead's, which was descended as far as the first belay at the top of the slab. We then traversed to the left by Jones and Collier's route as far as a pile of blocks. So far so good, but here the real difficulties began. The 'firma loca' of Jones' Deep Ghyll route was our immediate *objectif,* and was not really far distant, but some steep forbidding slabs barred the way. They were also rather slimy and moss covered. It was decided that one of us should make a trial trip across, and then report to the others. A descent of fifteen feet had first to be made down a three-step staircase, which, however, was tilted up at an unpleasant angle. All spare parts of my anatomy were brought into requisition here for clinging to the greasy slabs, and I was not sorry for the rope from above. Once down this portion, a horizontal traverse to the left over steep rocks had to be made to reach an obvious grassy ledge, from the further end of which a short mossy slab brought me up to a second grassy ledge just above the 'firma loca'. The first doubtful move in the game had therefore succeeded, and I wended my way back to the others, rejoicing. The whole party then made the passage, one by one, the last man using a doubled rope over an excellent belay above the pile of blocks. This section is perhaps the least pleasant on the whole Traverse. From the 'firma loca' we crossed over to the foot of the arête, where we rested, and refreshed the inner man before tackling the next section. This was the 100-foot descent to Hopkinson's Cairn. Down the first portion of this the last man again used the doubled rope, this time not merely as a comfort, but as a necessity – the rocks are scarcely climbable for fifteen feet. Sansom, who came last, swung down hand over hand in great style, while I made certainty doubly sure by belaying him from the further end of Hopkinson and Tribe's traverse. The rest of the descent to the Cairn did not delay us long, and we were soon pulling off our boots in preparation for crossing the Pinnacle Face. This is one of the most delightful sections of the whole expedition, but a knowledge of the place is desirable, otherwise much time may be wasted, as nail-marks are more or less absent. The descent is first made down the steep slab to the Moss Ledge. To reach the Waiting Room from here, two alternatives present themselves; firstly, one can descend to the Second Nest and follow Jones' route from there onwards, or, secondly, one can traverse more or less horizontally right across the face into Hopkinson's Gully, striking the latter at the point where Jones' route leaves it. This is then followed as before. In point of difficulty there is not much to choose between the two. On this occasion the first man went right to the top of the difficult portion of Jones' route before anybody followed, and this is probably the safest way of doing it for all concerned. The last man can use a doubled rope down the Slab if necessary, and this would be advisable if he is unacquainted with the place. When we had all got across and had put on our boots (which had been slung across on a rope), we lost no time in getting down into Steep Ghyll.

The next section of the Traverse, namely the crossing of Pisgah Buttress, now confronted us, and we were rather in doubt as to which was the best line to take. However, we soon espied a twenty-foot crack on the wall of the Buttress, rather below the point where we had entered the Ghyll. This proved amenable enough, and enabled us to get out on to the face of the Buttress about on the level of the Fives Court. This was about thirty feet to our left, and nature had been so kind as to provide a neat horizontal ledge just wide enough to enable one to edge along fairly comfortably, but scarcely with one's hands in one's pockets, and leading direct to the Court. It should be noted that we had to climb two or three feet upwards from the top of the crack to reach this ledge. From the Fives Court we descended into Moss Ghyll by the usual route.

We had now reached the Central Buttress, the crux of the climb.

Anyone examining a good photograph of Scafell face will notice a thin horizontal line crossing the Central Buttress about 100 feet above Rake's Progress. This appears to stretch right across as far as the more westerly of two well-defined slanting cracks. This line we held to be the solution of the problem. We were not without previous knowledge of the place, and knew how to reach it from Moss Ghyll. The latter we descended as far as the foot of the third pitch. Twenty feet below this a slanting grassy furrow starts from the Ghyll, cutting into the wall on the left. From the point mentioned, a beautiful horizontal traverse led into this furrow, which landed us, about twenty feet higher, at the right-hand extremity of the ledge across the Buttress. We could not as yet see right across, as a corner intervened ten feet beyond where we were, but once this had been rounded we had an uninterrupted view. The ledge on which we now stood is in many ways unique, and is certainly one of the most remarkable places in Cumberland. Above it, the wall of the Central Buttress rises sheer for several hundred feet, almost hopelessly smooth and steep, while there is a sufficiently precipitous drop down to Rake's Progress to make one move circumspectly. At the further end of the ledge Botterill's Slab shows its full height, and looks appallingly difficult. The part of the ledge where we now stood was comfortably broad – six feet or so – and we called it 'the Oval'. We now attempted to follow it to its extreme end, hoping thus to reach the foot of Botterill's Slab. I therefore moved along carefully to the left, for some distance without serious difficulty, but soon the width began to decrease until, at a point twenty-five feet short of the Slab, and sixty or seventy feet beyond the Oval, I felt that my balance was getting rather too delicate, and turned tail. There would have been no object in going on, moreover, as I could see that the ledge gradually tapered off to nothing several feet short of the Slab. It was now beginning to get dark, and it was therefore useless to attempt any further exploration, so we returned to Moss Ghyll by the way we had come, and thence valleywards. The next day was wet, but the day following was fine again, and we started at what, for us, was a really early hour – 8 a.m. It was our idea to see whether we could not make a traverse across the upper part of the Central Buttress, leaving, for the time being, the route we had previously tried. We therefore followed Moss Ghyll to the belay above the Collie step, from which point Sansom led us straight up the wall ahead, as far as a good grassy ledge which was to be our starting point for this section of the Traverse.

A most sensational corner was first rounded on unsatisfactory holds. Here the chief excitement was reserved for Brunskill, who came round last. He was wearing for the occasion a long female garment showing an elegant waist, which he had appropriated from the large collection of relics in Walker's Gully, and was the cause of much ribald laughter as he swung round the corner, his coat-tails flying in the air, over a drop worthy of the Dolomites. After moving along a little further over easy ground, we entered what is known as the Bayonet-shaped Crack. An inspection of the lower portion of this proving unsatisfactory, we were obliged to make an upward traverse to the left for seventy or eighty feet. Here Sansom made a daring descent of the face for nearly 100 feet. This, too, was fruitless, and moving still further to the left, we were gradually forced out on to the easy rocks at the top. There was nothing for it, therefore, but to return to the ledge lower down, which we had reached on the previous occasion.

Looking down over the edge of the Oval, we saw a narrow ledge thirty feet below, which seemed as if it might help us. It was, however, impossible to climb straight down, and we could find nothing suitable for doubling the rope round. But Gibson in the meantime had been doing a bit of gardening away on our left, disclosing an excellent belay, and, what was more, had found a feasible route down to the ledge. This was highly satisfactory. The belay was about twenty feet beyond the end of the Oval, and with the rope passed round it the descent was safely made. It was not really very difficult, but the last man thought it wise to run his rope through a loop. From the lower ledge to the foot of Botterill's Slab was now only a matter of a few feet, and though the start was awkward, we were soon across. It was already rather late in the day, and as we had still plenty of work before us, we decided it would save time if one of us went round by Keswick Brothers' Climb to the top of the Slab, and let down a rope for the others. As two of the party had climbed it a few days before, we thought ourselves justified in regarding it as done. This was, therefore, carried out, and we were soon re-united at the foot of Keswick Brothers' Pinnacle. Before further describing the Traverse, I would like to say a word regarding Botterill's Slab. The whole party was of the emphatic opinion that, as far as difficulty is concerned, it stands in a class by itself. For sixty feet the leader has no adequate resting-place, but must advance on holds which in several places are barely sufficient. I am convinced now that to attempt to lead up it without previous inspection would be unjustifiable.

We now descended Keswick Brothers' Climb as far as Collier's Ledge. An attempt to traverse horizontally from here proved quite unsuccessful, so we went to the top of the second pitch of Collier's Climb. Gibson now informed us that we could have reached this point by a traverse from the Pinnacle which he had made on a former occasion. We therefore mentally substituted this for the route we had taken, and again tried to work to the left. Sansom managed to traverse for thirty or forty feet, but was again obliged to give an unsatisfactory report. We therefore decided to waste no more time on it, as it was already beginning to get dusk, and finished up the left wall of the recess in which the final section of Collier's Climb lies.

We were thus unable to reach the Penrith Climb, but it will be seen from the photograph that the Traverse loses little by that.

On looking back on our two days' work, we came

to the conclusion that a party familiar with the route could finish it in from six to seven hours. There are about 1,600 feet of actual climbing, the standard of which is throughout remarkably high. The fact that Botterill's Slab is included is sufficient to prevent the Traverse as a whole from becoming in the least popular, but many parties would be satisfied with doing sections of it, i.e. the traverse of the Pinnacle, or that from Steep Ghyll to the foot of Botterill's Slab; the latter could be recommended to any strong and steady party containing no nervous members. Speaking for ourselves, we felt that the whole expedition, involving as it does much more than mere technical ability, ranks as one of the finest in Britain.

FRCC Journal, Vol II No 3, 1912

G.R Dale. Sept '04

One outcome of the exploration that resulted in the successful girdle traverse of the cliff was that Herford and Sansom had a pretty good understanding of what lay above and below the unclimbed middle section of the central buttress. They also knew that time and weather had split a great flake of rock from the main face and this flake linked the extremities of previous exploration. In addition, individual boulders had become trapped in the resultant crevice. It was the existence of this feature and its potential resting places that persuaded them that this might be the chink in an otherwise impenetrable armour.

There was, first, a number of mind games that had to be played. Despite its imposing position halfway up a 400-foot cliff, it was possible they could persuade themselves that the ascent of the Flake was not dissimilar to the difficult outcrop problems that Herford had successfully tackled in the Peak District. It was about the height of an average gritstone edge. The Oval, if not terra firma, was sufficiently large to allow a group of climbers to assemble and collaborate in a joint assault and, once the top of the Flake had been grasped, it was possible to 'walk off'

via Jeffcoat's Ledge. All that remained was getting Herford from bottom to top.

The solution was a curious mixture of ancient and modern. The modern was a thorough investigation of the problem from above, presumably involving the necessary 'gardening'. The ancient was to minimise a long and dangerous run-out by splitting the pitch into as many subsections as possible, and to overcome holdless rock through the use of the human pyramid. The subsequent guidebook to the climb explains. The second climbs the easy section (twenty-five feet) to the first chockstone. The leader climbs past his second to the second chockstone, where he ties on. The second climbs on to the highest point of the leader's anatomy (twenty-five feet), whence, if sufficiently tall, he can reach the top of the Flake (fifteen feet). Straightforward enough, but one is left with the feeling that this was less a description of how to do it than a report on how it was done.

Eventually, on April 20th 1914, a party of four pushed and pulled itself from the foot of the Flake to the safety of Jeffcoat's Ledge. Two days later, a way was found on the upper part of the face. All the pieces of the jigsaw were at hand and it was the intention of those involved to return in September to climb the route in one go. But more pressing matters threatened and the young men who had struggled in the intimidating space that overhangs Hollow Stones would soon be occupied by the greater trials of Ypres and the Somme.

Scafell Central Buttress

G S Sansom, 1914

Some two years ago, Herford and I, in an inquisitive
spirit, climbed up a grassy scoop leading out of Moss
Ghyll on to the Central Buttress. We did not seriously
believe that we should find a new climb on this rock
face, for it appears to be singularly unbroken and
almost vertical for over 200 feet. It was, however, an
unknown region, and as such appealed to us.

The scoop was not very difficult and we were
soon looking around a corner at the top along a narrow grassy ledge which apparently extended right
across the face to Botterill's Slab. The rocks fell away
very steeply below and a sheer smooth wall rose up
to a great height above: its regularity was interrupted
at one point, it is true, by an enormous rock flake
which tapered out to nothing seventy feet higher.
For some obscure reason this ledge suggested vague
possibilities, which we did not fully appreciate at
the time. The Great Flake looked quite hopeless as
a means of ascent and we dismissed the idea at once
and concentrated our attention on the Moss Ghyll

side of the buttress, which was broken up by right-angled corners running upwards from west to east at a uniform angle of sixty-five degrees. The nearest of these corners stopped us in less than thirty feet, but we determined to try the next. It appeared difficult of access from this ledge: accordingly a descent to the Ghyll, and an awkward traverse from the top of the next pitch was effected. I climbed up this groove with some difficulty until the slab on the left almost gave out and upward progress seemed scarcely feasible; the groove immediately on my right continued upwards for a considerable distance, but the traverse into it appeared too difficult and I returned to Herford. We thereupon decided to give up the attempt and climb Pisgah Buttress instead. We did so, with searching eyes on the rock face which had so successfully repulsed us, and I for one returned to Wastdale with the opinion that Central Buttress would not go.

That day's work was not, however, wasted, for it led indirectly to the discovery of the Girdle Traverse, inasmuch as it apparently demonstrated the possibility of reaching Botterill's Slab from Moss Ghyll and thus overcoming the most serious obstacle to the expedition. Some three months later Herford made the second ascent of Botterill's Slab, and a few days afterwards the Girdle Traverse was completed. My belief, that the ledge on the Central Buttress actually joined the Slab, was founded on insufficient data, and the credit for the discovery of a feasible connection between the two is due to H B Gibson.

Consideration of other climbs, which led up apparently impossible but actually feasible rocks, impressed on us the necessity of not judging by appearances, but of trying all places, however impossible or impracticable they looked. The proverb 'Better is the sight of the eyes than the wandering of the desire' is inimical to those desirous of finding new routes on a much-explored rock face. We accordingly assured one another that, as we had not actually attempted the ascent of the Great Flake, there was still a chance of finding a feasible route up the Central Buttress.

It was not until June, 1913, that we had an opportunity of putting this theory into practice on the Central Buttress. It is however one thing to talk lightheartedly of trying to climb a narrow forty-foot crack, of which the top overhangs the bottom some twelve feet, and quite another thing to stand at its foot prepared to do so. The crack proper started some thirty feet above our grass ledge (the Oval) and obviously could be reached without great difficulty. I ascended about twenty-five feet and found myself below a large bulge in the side of the flake; I could have got over this bulge, but the sight of the crack above was too much for me, and Herford took my place and climbed to the foot of the crack. He also decided that to attempt to force it, without knowledge as to what lay above, would be unjustifiable.

I was abroad all that summer, but Herford and Jeffcoat spent a profitable afternoon in exploration from above. From the top of Keswick Brothers' Climb – below the variation finish – they traversed out on to the face of the Central Buttress, first downwards some thirty feet, and then horizontally to the right for about the same distance to a large flat rock, the Cannon, which is a conspicuous feature in the profile view of the face. From this point they descended a narrow shattered ridge for forty feet to a good belay on an exposed platform known as Jeffcoat's Ledge, and a further descent of twelve feet gave access to a shelf of rock some three feet wide proximally, narrowing gradually down to eighteen inches and supporting various large rock flakes in a state of doubtful equilibrium. Distally the ledge was concealed by a rather larger detached flake some ten feet high and barely three inches wide at the top. Herford traversed out on the ledge, climbed on to this detached mass, walked along it and climbed down the opposite side. He now realised that he was on the top of the Great Flake, which formed the left retaining wall of the crack we had tried to climb from below. The flake narrowed down to a knife-edge, so thin and fretted that it was actually perforated in some places. Crawling carefully along it to the end, Herford descended the overhanging crack, whilst Jeffcoat paid out rope from the belay. Unfortunately the rope jammed during the descent and Herford had very great difficulty in getting down. He considered, however, that the crack was just climbable, and wrote me to that effect. Thus ended what is probably one of the most remarkable and bold explorations ever carried out in the district, and it is to be greatly regretted that Jeffcoat, who had lent such valuable assistance, was unable to join us in the actual ascent of the climb.

On April 19th of this year Herford, Gibson, Holland and myself repaired to Scafell for the attempt. Herford and Gibson ascended Keswick Brothers' Climb and traversed out on to the Central Buttress, whilst Holland and I climbed direct from Rake's Progress to the Oval. Gibson lowered me a rope down the crack and after removing my boots I attempted the ascent. As far as the bulge, above-mentioned, the climbing was comparatively simple, but from this point to a large jammed stone twenty feet higher it was extremely difficult, as the crack is practically holdless and just too wide to permit a secure arm wedge. Two fairly good footholds permit of a position of comparative comfort just below the jammed stone and I noted, as Herford had suggested, that it was possible to thread a rope there. The stone itself afforded quite a good handhold, but the crack above overhung to such a shocking extent that the ascent of the remaining twelve feet proved excessively difficult. My arms gave out long before the top was reached and a very considerable amount of pulling from Gibson was required before I joined him. Herford then tried the ascent on a rope and just succeeded in getting up without assistance. We thereupon decided to attempt the ascent in the ortho-dox manner, and preparatory thereto descended by Broad Stand and rejoined Holland on the Oval.

Our plan of attack was to climb up the crack and thread a loop behind the jammed stone, and I undertook to do this if Herford would lead the upper part, which he was quite prepared to do. My first procedure was to soak two feet of the end of a rope in wet moss, to render it stiff and facilitate the threading. I then attempted the ascent, but six feet below the jammed stone found my position too precarious to be pleasant and called to Herford for a shoulder. He came up without the least hesitation and standing on the bulge at the foot of the crack, steadied my feet on small holds until I attained a safer position and was able to climb up to the chockstone. The stiff rope threaded very easily, and making a double loop I ran my own rope through it for the descent, which was, under those conditions, quite safe.

After a brief rest Herford tied on to the threaded rope and speedily reached the level of the chockstone. He made a splendid effort to climb the upper part, but his strength gave out and he returned for a rest. A second equally fine effort was also unsuccessful, and he climbed down to the Oval. I then made one attempt, but soon abandoned it, and we unanimously agreed to postpone the ascent till the morrow, leaving the threaded rope *in situ*. As Holland had already spent *seven* hours on the Oval we decided to waste no more time, and accordingly descended via the traverse into Moss Ghyll.

The next day we climbed to the Oval direct from the Progress and one member ascended to the chockstone to renew the loop, which showed slight signs of wear from the previous day's use. We decided that combined tactics would be necessary, and accordingly ran a second rope through the loop. Herford tied on one rope and I on the other, whilst Gibson and Holland manipulated the respective ropes. I followed Herford closely up the crack and hung on to the loop whilst he used my shoulders as footholds. Directly he vacated them I climbed three feet higher and hung by my hands from the top of the chockstone, whilst he again employed me as footholds, which are most sorely needed at this point, for the crack is practically holdless and overhangs about twenty degrees. A minute or two of severe struggling and he reached the top – to the great joy of all members of the party.

Herford thoughtfully hung a short loop over the tip of the flake to assist us in the ascent, but even then we required much help from above, and it was with a sense of great relief that we found ourselves on the crest of the flake. Murray, who had been observing us from the recess with some interest, was delighted with an invitation to join the party, so we lowered him a rope down the crack and induced him to remove the threaded loop on the way up.

We were well satisfied with the day's work, but not with the climb, inasmuch as it left 150 feet of the Central Buttress still unclimbed. Two days later, therefore, we set out, greatly regretting Gibson's absence from the party, to explore the upper part of the face.

Fifty feet above the top of the Great Flake on the Central Buttress is an irregular V-shaped grass ledge, from the western end of which springs a wide chimney, which is the lower section of a conspicuous Bayonet-shaped Crack, running up to the very top of the crags. The upper section of this crack was, we knew, easy; the lower portion looked very unpleasant, but we hoped to avoid it by climbing the steep face on the left. With Holland and Slater belaying us, we climbed down steep rocks to the V-shaped ledge 100 feet below, and from there were able to look down a remarkably smooth and almost vertical wall to the top of the Great Flake, fifty feet lower. The wall was broken at one point by a right-angled arête, which, in spite of the fact that it overhung slightly, possessed sufficiently good holds to permit of a comfortable descent of twenty-five feet. From its foot a wonderfully exposed traverse across the almost vertical face on the left enabled us to pass behind a large detached pinnacle and climb slightly downwards to the shattered ridge against the foot of which the Great Flake abuts.

Much elated at this discovery we climbed back to Holland and Slater, and the three of us at once descended the easy rocks to the Cannon. Belayed from this point I led across the traverse and up to the V ledge. Herford then took the lead, Holland going second. Now the way by which we had descended necessitated an extremely difficult hand traverse, on bad holds, in an exposed situation, and we therefore cast about for a better route. Herford first tried the Bayonet-shaped Crack, but it looked repulsively difficult and he abandoned it in favour of a most exhilarating traverse across its foot, on to the vertical wall beyond, and upwards across the latter for thirty feet to a steep slab, which he followed, for another twenty-five feet, to a good belay at the top of the lower section of the crack. We soon joined him here and climbed easily up the left wall of the upper portion of the Bayonet-shaped Crack to the top of the Crags.

The Central Buttress climb as a whole is extremely interesting and the situations absolutely unique. As regards difficulty: the direct ascent to the Oval from Rake's Progress is decidedly difficult and entails an eighty-foot run-out. The Flake Crack is unfortunately excessively severe and requires very careful management to render its ascent safe. The traverses and ascents on the upper wall are extraordinarily exposed, but not unduly severe, and the climbing is exceedingly enjoyable. The climb is certainly the longest in the district.

Note: *Owing to the unforeseen events of this summer it has not been possible to bring this account up to date. We hoped to repeat the ascent this September, including in it a new and improved start, which has been proved feasible but has not at present been climbed throughout. It affords a more direct route to the Oval and is of first rate quality. Better photographs were to have been taken and further explorations carried out.*

FRCC Journal, Vol III, No 2, 1914

Seven years were to elapse before the climb was repeated and it is interesting to speculate what delayed the second ascent. The most obvious reason is the intervention of the First World War, which consumed a considerable chunk of the hiatus. But the war did not mean that climbing in the area ceased altogether. There were a dozen new routes recorded within the duration and there must have been ambitious climbers, involved locally in the shipbuilding and chemical industries, who were exempt from active service.

Nor does this explain the apparent lack of ambition in the immediate post-war years. As with Botterill's Slab, it may have been that the route was technically too difficult and psychologically too intimidating for those who immediately followed. Of those with first-hand knowledge, only Holland remained. Herford and Jeffcoat had been killed in the war and Sansom, although he continued to climb, was now married and had lost interest in further exploration. On the other hand, H M Kelly, with Holland as second, put up a series of routes on Gable and Pillar in the immediate post-war years that were of the same order of difficulty.

There again, perhaps Kelly had wanted to do it but was unable to muster a sufficiently strong party to make a serious bid. At least one other member of the party would have had to have been capable of either leading up to and tying on to the chockstone or, alternatively, tackling the final fifteen feet without the protection of a rope from above. Holland was available. But the memories surrounding his own ascent would not have necessarily encouraged another attempt.

Moreover, there may have been more to the procrastination than merely climbing matters. The recent hard climbs on Scafell, culminating in the successful assault on its central buttress, were irrevocably linked with Siegfried Herford and it may be that his death in 1916 gave them a further significance. There is no doubt that Herford, physically striking and outstandingly talented, was held in equal measures of awe and affection by all who knew him. Keith Treacher's finely researched biography* contains a series of tributes sent to Herford's parents after his death. As one, they praise the man as well as the climber and the appreciation is, perhaps, most succinctly summed up in a sentence by Geoffrey

* *Siegfried Herford, An Edwardian Rock Climber,* K Treacher, 2000.

Winthrop Young: 'Siegfried was for us – besides being himself – the greatest rock climbing figure perhaps of all time: in his life already a tradition.'

Nor was it just the loss of Herford that hit so cruelly at the members of the Fell & Rock. Of the sixty-eight club members who had seen active service, nearly thirty percent were never to return and the Club must have been shaken to its core by the dreadful scale of the loss. Those who remained must have felt that some gesture had to be made and plans were laid to purchase some part of the Lakes to act as a permanent memorial. This proved more difficult than had been anticipated. An offer to buy Pillar Rock was turned down by Lord Lonsdale, and an attempt to buy Napes Needle failed because the owner was only willing to sell if a large parcel of unaffordable land was included in the deal.

It was not until 1924 that negotiations with a new owner were finally successful and a memorial tablet could be placed on the summit of Great Gable. In the intervening six years, there may have been a sense of unease that there was no apparent token of remembrance for those who had fallen and it is possible that Herford's last climb might have, consciously or unconsciously, become such a symbol. Indeed, the idea was implied in Laycock's obituary on the death of his great friend and climbing partner.

The mountains themselves are monuments to him, their favourite child – though Scafell may rightly grudge to the other hills an equal share of the honour. *

It would be an easy step for the Club members to single out CB, as the apotheosis for *their* favourite child.

And there would be a logic to it. Unlike other great Lakeland rock faces, only the central buttress of Scafell contained a unique climb unconfused by inferior variants. There must have been a sense of great parochial pride that the Club had instigated the ascent of 'one of the most difficult climbs in the world'. But, perhaps overall, the seizing upon the route as an icon fulfilled a more subtle need. Once the war had ended, reasons were sought for the apparently pointless carnage. The question being addressed was – if God was to be thanked for matching us with His hour, what did He have in mind exactly?

Those who had witnessed the events at first hand knew that the early rhetoric did not match the substance, and the likes of Siegfried Sassoon and Robert

* *FRCC Journal,* 1916.

Graves were not afraid to say so. To them, it was less a just and noble struggle against the AntiChrist, more a struggle to survive in the face of incompetence and personal bewilderment. Whether it was Sassoon's scarlet Majors, who sped 'glum heroes up the line to death',* or 'The inward scream, the duty to run mad'† of Graves that best sums up the chaos is difficult to say, but it was clear to one and all that whatever the point of dying for one's country was, Dulce et Decorum non erat.

An answer was to be suggested by Wilfred Owen, the finest of the war poets. Initially, in poems like 'The Chances' and 'Anthem for Doomed Youth', he had followed the same withering satirical line of attack adopted by his mentor, Sassoon. However, in 'Futility', sickened at the loss of yet another young life, he bitterly concludes by questioning as to 'what made fatuous sunbeams toil/To break earth's sleep at all?' and it was his desire to be remembered as a poet rather than a polemicist that persuaded him to pursue this line of thought.

In 'Strange Meeting', Owen, amongst other matters, examines the possibility that the sacrifice was not along national lines, as had been assumed, but

* 'Base Details'   † 'Recalling War'

that a huge swath of youth from all the European nations had been collectively cut down for some greater purpose. The poem with its paradoxical 'I am the enemy you killed, my friend' and the time-embracing 'Whatever hope is yours/Was my life also' underlines this unity. The selfless death of so many was, so some hoped, the ultimate sacrificial act that might purge 'with truths that lie too deep for taint' the self-styled civilised world of its imperial vanities.

Siegfried Herford, part English, part German, described by the *Manchester Guardian* as 'a man of beautiful character and great gifts' would have been an epitome of such an ideal. If his monument was Central Buttress, then a second ascent might have been viewed by some as akin to 'Whipplesnaith' and his Cambridge night-climbers placing a chamber pot on the top of the Cenotaph. Of course, this sentiment would not have been universally held and in 1921 a member of the Yorkshire Ramblers' Club duly made the second ascent. The official response of the Fell & Rock can be gauged by the tone of the following article written by C F Holland.

The Great Central Buttress of Scafell

C F Holland, 1921

Some few years ago, in 1913 to be exact, tired, dirty and dishevelled, I climbed wearily into one of the antique carriages that convey one from Bangor to Bethesda.

Opposite me sat a tall young man of striking appearance, obviously alien in every way to the quarrymen and suchlike who filled the carriage, jabbering some strange language, presumably Welsh. According to the usual custom of the English under such conditions we did not exchange a single word, but when on reaching Bethesda we found we were both bound for Ogwen we agreed to share a vehicle, and the subsequent conversation that enlivened the somewhat slow progress to the cottage inaugurated a friendship that is now only a fragrant memory. My companion was S W Herford. The next day, my first with him in the mountains, showed me that I had met a man of highly unusual personality, initiative, and physical strength, while the masterly way in which he led the Western Gully on the Glyder Fawr demonstrated his superb qualities as a cragsman. Next day, his party arrived, and the good-natured refusal to allow me to stand out proved the thoughtful kindness and unselfishness that were so remarkable and engaging a part of his character.

The next evening at Ogwen was one to remember.

All the rest had retired to bed, and I alone remained, reading and trying to cultivate a mood propitiatory to the Goddess of Sleep, when suddenly the stillness of the night was broken by uproar, obviously proceeding from the room overhead. Loud and continued bumpings of some heavy object were followed by yells and noises as of a large bundle of carpet being rolled about. A particularly loud shout was followed by a piercing scream, after which Homeric roars of laughter, gradually dying away till silence reigned once more. In the morning I collected from the various members of the party the meaning of these nocturnal disturbances. It seems that four of them were sharing a room, and that Herford was sharing a bed with one who desired to have a more than his fair share of the bedclothes. On being expostulated with, the other man had refused to yield any portion of what he had acquired, and was promptly thrown on to the floor, albeit carrying with him the bedclothes entire, purporting, I imagine, to sleep where he lay. Thereupon, Herford twisted his toes, to induce him to part with the integuments (I am not quite sure of this word, but it sounds good), in which he had now wound himself after the fashion of a cocoon. In its agony, the cocoon rolled about; hence the bumpings, and eventually went under one of the beds. Now it so chanced that it was the bed of one who had acquired the strange habit of placing his false teeth under his bed. Hence the loud shout, as he sprang forth to rescue his property from their imminent danger, while the final dominating scream emanated from the cocoon, who had apparently been severely bitten.

But Wales is not Cumberland, and as the heading of this article announces that it is about the Great Central Buttress of Scafell, it will perhaps be as well to start writing about it.

My acquaintance with this extraordinarily perpendicular cliff was made in January, 1914, when, one snowy afternoon, four of us, with Herford as leader, traversed out from the sheltered recesses of Moss Ghyll on to the great ledge that runs across the buttress some eighty to 100 feet above Lord's Rake.

Under the prevailing conditions, the expedition

seemed to me a most perilous one, and the two corners we had to pass places of some severity, easy as they may be on a hot summer's day.

Eventually we reached the belay near the end of the ledge, and prepared to rope down. As a matter of fact, Herford climbed down successfully, in spite of the snow, though he announced that it was pretty near the limit. When the third man had joined me at the belay, I told him I was going down strictly on the rope, and, without waiting to ascertain whether he was ready for me or not, seized the rope with both hands, and more or less jumped over the edge.

As he was not ready, my descent was a remarkably rapid one, till I came to a stop some twenty-five feet lower with my feet on a ledge, or, as Archer Thomson would have put it, 'chanced on a knob of rock'. It will always be a proud memory that my ejaculation during this unexpected performance was 'God Save the King.' There are so many things one might have said and regretted. A little while previously I had surveyed in the gathering gloom the crack which was pointed out as a possible means by which the buttress might be ascended above the Oval, and summarily decided that it was impossible. Near Easter, however, I found to my horror that a serious attack on the buttress was contemplated, and that the attempt was to be made, not tentatively – there was little of the tentative in Herford's character – but with determination to succeed, if human beings could do so.

The snows of March had disappeared, and the weather conditions were perfect, when, a few days later, Herford, Sansom, Gibson, and myself set out on what I imagined to be a day of preliminary exploration, but which subsequently resolved itself into a sustained effort to climb the appallingly difficult middle section of the buttress.

The plan of campaign was as follows: Sansom led me up to the great ledge, the widest section of which is the Oval, while Herford and Gibson went up Keswick Brothers, and down the steep groove, a junior Botterill's slab, that leads to the singular horizontal portion of the crack, ending abruptly in a vertical dive of seventy feet to the Oval. From the end of the crack a rope was lowered, and on this Sansom went up the crack, his strength apparently giving out about ten feet from the top. For some seven hours I sat solitary on the ledge, and smoked peacefully, an experience that has given me my appreciation of and sympathy with the feelings of the well-known pelican in the wilderness; voices were occasionally wafted by the breeze from above, but no sight of my companions was vouchsafed until late afternoon, when they rejoined me on the Oval, and made preparations to climb the crack.

The first job was to put a thread round the lower part of the great stone jammed in the crack some fifty or more feet above the ledge.

Sansom went aloft to do this, but had not reached the stone when he appeared to be in difficulties, and shortly announced that his position was insecure.

One of my most vivid memories of Herford is that of the way in which he went up to Sansom's assistance, climbing at a great speed, and, to all appearances, lying on the rope as he climbed.

As soon as Herford had reached him, I expected to see Sansom beat a retreat at once, but, to my mingled admiration and astonishment, he went higher, using Herford's shoulders to stand on. The thread, a double loop, was satisfactorily fixed, and the two came down to the Oval again. After a brief rest both Sansom and then Herford had a shot at the crack, but they were both too tired with the previous exploration to push the final overhanging section, and at last abandoned the effort, though obviously with extreme reluctance. Much useful work had been done, however, and ultimate success was now deemed reasonably likely, given complete physical freshness and combined tactics under perfect weather conditions.

The season was the finest April I ever remember, and the next day was absolutely perfect, a happy augury that was justified by the event. By eleven we were all on the Oval, and preparations were being carried on for the great ascension.

Sansom employed himself in soaking the end of a rope in wet moss to facilitate the threading necessary while the loops were being renewed. The latter was considered advisable, to make the attempt as safe as possible. He then carried out this difficult and arduous task, and all was ready.

Herford and Sansom went up again, the former using the latter's shoulders to conserve his strength for the exceptional physical exertion entailed by the last twelve feet, while Gibson and I held their ropes, running through the double thread, a job which engaged all our attention, and prevented us from watching our companions as they climbed.

I think the first sign of success was a cry from Gibson of 'He's up,' and looking up I saw Herford lying exhausted at the top of the crack, supported by his jammed right knee. It seemed but a little while, so great was the relief after the previous tension, which we now fully realised, before Sansom and Gibson were both up the crack also, and I was left, forlorn and frightened, ready to give all my worldly wealth to avoid what lay before me. Over the ensuing struggles I will draw a veil; suffice it to say that I had two ropes on, and climbed up a third, failed miserably to cut away the thread as I was asked to do, and finished in a state of utter exhaustion, after a wild haul at a knotted loop that Herford had with characteristic thoughtfulness placed in just the right position. Here we were joined by Murray, who had reached the Oval on his own. And so, leisurely up the groove to the Cannon, and a prolonged rest at the top of the crags. No further climbing took place that day, as we were all very tired, and after what had been done anything else would have been anti-climax. Sansom's photo of the party at rest is one that brings back the happiest of all my climbing memories.

A most remarkable incident had occurred while the crack was being led. Sansom was hanging on by indifferent sloping handholds on or near the lower end of the great chockstone, and Herford was standing on his shoulders, about to make the first step of the last tremendous solo effort. The initial difficulty confronting him was that of getting a purchase with his left foot in a groove unsuitably shaped for that purpose. Sansom's left hand began to slip under the great strain, and must inevitably have given way very soon, in which case he would have come off, though only for a foot or two, on to the loops. Herford's fall, unavoidable if this had happened, would have been a very serious affair indeed, and even if his rope had held it is impossible to see how we below could have given any assistance, beyond keeping the ropes tight, if either had been injured in any way.

At this moment, however, the great Goddess of Luck took a hand in the game. I call it 'Luck'; there are those who would name it differently.

Finding himself unable to get his foot as he wanted it, Herford stepped back and accidentally put his foot on the slipping hand, thus holding it in position; and the difficult step was made so quickly at the second attempt that Sansom was able to support the double weight till that of the leader was removed. So it may well be said that 'Luck' was a sixth member of the party, and no inefficient one either.

To me it now seemed that the Central Buttress had been conquered, and that all was over bar the shouting, but our insatiable leaders were still not satisfied, as they considered that the buttress had been little more than half-climbed, leaving some 150 to 200 feet of the upper part as yet untouched.

So, two days later, we set out again, this time unfortunately without Gibson, but with Slater to take his place. After going up Moss Ghyll, Slater and I held ropes, while the others explored possibilities. After a couple of hours they rejoined us, and described how they had reached a fair ledge, now named the V ledge, some fifty feet above the great Flake. This ledge they had reached before from the groove leading to the Cannon, and the only thing that now remained was to go and do the whole upper section of the climb from below. And so to the Cannon and down the groove. Here, as the weak member of the party, I was roped up in the centre. My recollection of the ensuing fifty feet is of a very difficult balance traverse, in an extremely exposed position, to a pinnacle, followed by a rather easier traverse to an open chimney, exceptionally vertical, but with good holds, leading to the V ledge.

A later recollection of the same place is that the first traverse is not so hard as I had thought, and that the second section is impossible, as it leads across a vertical wall with no holds. In any case, neither Crawford nor myself could make anything of it whatsoever. The place is one where to lead is definitely much harder than following, owing to the very high degree of exposure. Once on the V ledge, it seemed that all was over, but the buttress still had something to say on the subject, and put up a magnificent fight right to the finish; and indeed it was anybody's game to the bitter end; bitter indeed for Sansom, as it was the last climb he ever had with Herford, though there is some comfort in the thought that it was for both of them the climax of achievement; as far as rock climbing is concerned, that is to say: for Herford, the crowning achievement was yet to come.

The difficulty that now arose was that a hand traverse on sloping holds some fifteen feet above the ledge, quite feasible for a roped descent, was too risky a lead from a ledge inadequately supplied with belays; there are several belays at the right hand end of the ledge, but they are too far away from the pitch. After this disappointment, a new exit had to be found, and a likely looking groove on the left was tried, but proved quite hopeless after a cursory inspection; also, it was still further from the belays than the route originally selected. The right hand end of the ledge now came in for attention; it is the broadest part, and the belay problem is easily solved. This end is enclosed by a retaining wall. Above is the lower part of the Bayonet-shaped Crack. A rift or chimney in this retaining wall slopes down at an angle of forty-five degrees, and looking down it one sees Hollow Stones, very far down indeed!

Herford was still leading, and was entirely off the ground previously explored. The position we were now in was decidedly interesting. We had apparently reached an impasse, and any solution was bound to be severely sensational, for the alternative to ascent, a very airy business, was a descent down the chimney and along the traverses, a course that did not appeal to me in the least. The Bayonet-shaped Crack was obviously the next thing to try, but after getting up a dozen feet or so Herford announced that it was too difficult, nor could he break over the corner on to the vertical face beyond.

The hand traverse loomed up once more as a possible necessity, and my private impression is that it would have been pushed if no other option had offered itself, but it was very much a last and rather desperate resource.

One possible exit yet remained untried, and that

was down the rift in the retaining wall. It seemed rather hopeless, but in rock climbing one never knows till one gets to grips with things. Herford wriggled down the rift, blocked the exit for a bit, disappeared, the rope went out steadily, and within a couple of minutes a call came for me to follow. Wonderingly I did so. The rift was completely safe till one came to the end of it, and then one apparently came to space, and rather too much of it. In fact, considerable faith was needed to believe that a road went that way. However, it proved not a very difficult task to worm one's self out of the bottom of the chimney, and gain a stance on the wall outside.

It is to this place, that all the other situations on the climb lead. It is the culminating point of a series of positions whose exposure has to be seen to be believed, and the next fifty feet up the customary vertical wall, and this time on a ledge that overhangs Lord's Rake 300 feet below (a conservative estimate) are the absolute limit, so far as my knowledge of English crags goes, in the way of exposure.

Luckily, the holds are excellent, and the climbing is not very difficult. Eventually Sansom joined us, only the easier half of the Bayonet-shaped Crack remained, and the climb was over; the Great Central

Buttress had really fallen at last.

So far, writing the account of this great climb has been both an easy and a pleasurable task, but now I come to the difficult part. It must be quite plain that this article is mainly written as a panegyric of Herford. I want to say exactly what I think about him, and I don't think I can do better than repeat what I wrote originally: 'He will live in my memory as the finest and bravest man I have ever known'; and, I should like to add: 'Alive he had no equal, dead his supremacy is still unchallenged.'

There is something more that I wish to say about him, and the pith of it is contained in a poem written by an officer who later fell in Gallipoli. A copy of it was cut out of *The Times*, and sent to me when in France. It was with me through all the troublous times that followed, and lies before me now. The poet starts by describing his longing for Cumberland, and the wild beauty of the mountains; his desire to climb among them once again, and see 'Ridge and hollow rolling under to the fringes of the world.' He then voices the happiness of those who understand the meaning of Death:

Die, and feel their embers quicken,
Year by year, in summer time;

When the cotton grasses thicken,
On the hills they used to climb.

Follows the wondering thought as to whether he will die in England, or never return.

The concluding verse reminds me irresistibly of the close of some great fugue by Bach. Behind the quietude and calm certainty that all is well is to be felt a great surging wave of triumph, the triumph of final victory, and its reward of everlasting peace; where

The Light

Returning, shall give back the golden hours,
Ocean a windless level, Earth a lawn,
Spacious and full of sunlit dancing-places.

Thus Rupert Brooke. The man I am quoting phrases it as follows:

We shall pass in summer weather
We shall come at eventide,
Where the fells stand up together
And all quiet things abide;
Mixed with cloud and wind and river,
Sundistilled in dew and rain,
One with Cumberland for ever,
We shall go not forth again.

I, at any rate, firmly believe that the spirit of Herford is still abroad among the hills, and I know that some day I shall meet him there.

FRCC Journal, Vol V, No 3, 1921

Whether it was practical or sentimental considerations that had delayed a further ascent, the second ascensionist was well equipped to overcome them. For a start, he was an outstanding climber. Fergus Graham describes his first meeting with him:

> *I well remember C F Frankland's descent from his Yorkshire Olympus at Almscliffe to the rocks of Laddow. The occasion had all the atmosphere of a visit by royalty. It was a tremendous privilege for me to climb with him, though I am bound to admit that that is rather a euphemism. He led up the North Wall to the top and then brought up George Bower who in turn brought me up. Still, I saw him climbing at close quarters, and it was an education I never forgot.**

Frankland was also gritstone-trained and had developed the use of rubbers rather than stockinged feet for the more delicate sections. He was used to long run-outs with little or no protection and was as happy descending as ascending. (He chose, for example, to do the Girdle Traverse of Scafell the unorthodox way round, which meant climbing

* *High Peak*, Byne & Sutton, 1966.

down rather than up Botterill's Slab.) It is also clear from his second's account that he seriously considered climbing the Flake in one go, using the chock as a runner rather than a point of aid.

Second, as a member of the Yorkshire Ramblers' Club, he would be less susceptible to the sentiments of Holland than the Wasdale Head regulars. In fact, it is interesting to compare the ways in which the last and next articles are written. While the nature of Holland's admiration is unambiguous, there is, perhaps, a gentle mocking in Frankland's assessment of previous giants. The tone, also, is of a different order. The climbing of CB to Holland was a romantic epic. The dragon was slayed by the heroic courage and selfless quickwittedness of the protagonists. Whereas Frankland is more concerned to inform the reader about the relevance of rock strata in assisting or defying the climber's efforts and a few of the finer points on the art of rope management.

And Frankland's ascent probably had a significant effect on post-war climbing. If Scafell wasn't impregnable, then what was? Botterill had lifted the latch. Herford had opened the door. But Frankland placed down the welcome mat. New very severe climbs sprang up, if not like Hydra's heads at least with regularity, on the various Lakeland cliffs and Jones' registry of Exceptionally Severe Courses which 'the novice must on no account attempt' became the hit list for all aspiring leaders.

Novel Tactics on the Central Buttress, Scawfell

C D Frankland, 1922

Many years ago there was kept at Wastdale, in the hotel, a large manuscript book, in which new climbs could be entered. This valuable collection of information was freely used, and the volume has long since been filled from cover to cover. Its popularity has occasioned its undoing. Whole pages have mysteriously vanished, the most valuable being the first to go. The depredations of collectors only ceased when the proprietor wisely put away the battered, time-stained remains in his office. There is still a book, but it is only available to members of a kindred club. Should the suggested affiliation of clubs be brought about, one of its advantages might be in the pooling of records in a book open to all. Then there would be less excuse for not keeping up to date with the latest developments of our art, even for such as myself and others, who are not members of the club-with-the-book. And such a question as – 'What is this Central Buttress?' would not be asked. I felt some indignation at the lack of interest in recent exploration revealed by the question, until I remembered that a very few months ago I was ignorant that the crag east of Moss Ghyll had been so named.

The first reference to the Central Buttress in the private book is brief. It runs – 'Attempt on CB ('nuff said)' and occurs between two very fine achievements – Scawfell Pinnacle from Lord's Rake, by Hopkinson's Gully to Hopkinson's Cairn (first ascent GSS), and Girdle Traverse of Scawfell (second time). In order to explain the middle, cryptic entry it may be expanded into – 'An attempt on the Central Buttress, Scawfell, was frustrated by the unspeakable difficulties encountered.' Then its true relation to the other notes will be appreciated, and it will be a fair inference that something unusual in the way of severity is to be expected on the Central Buttress. The next reference, verbose in comparison, is dated 20th April, 1914. It reads – 'Scawfell Central Buttress, First Ascent, S W Herford, G S Sansom, H B Gibson, C F Holland.' The *Journal of the Fell and Rock Climbing Club* (Vol. III, No. 2) contains the thrilling story. Three strenuous days were needed to work out the details of the route, but the whole, direct ascent in one expedition was not accomplished as had been hoped. War broke out in the summer.

There are some things that even the War did not change, and one is the crag of Scawfell, where, in 1921, the great buttress still challenged the climbers to repeat the ascent of 1914. The new school of experts has concentrated its accumulated skill upon rock faces. Many startling routes have been forced up various astoundingly holdless walls. Meanwhile our old guidebooks are rapidly receding into 'back numbers'. The muscular methods of Owen Glynne Jones are discussed with a tolerant smile. The human ladder of his time finds no place in the tactics of to-day. Like Jones, our experts climb without boots, but out of respect for present-day social amenities, they hide their socks inside rubber shoes. Perhaps the tendency is to specialise too much on smooth faces to maintain the old skill of attack in what have been called 'the less important things of modern rock climbing,' such as chimneys and cracks. For the particular difficulty, which has defied the assaults of the new school, is one of these 'less important things', a comparatively small crack. It is gratifying to be able to say that our modern experts have resisted the temptation to follow the precedent established under similar conditions in Moss Ghyll.

At Wastdale in the summer, an after-supper stroll

down by the lake is a popular feature of the daily programme, and, arrived at the head of Wastwater, we find an antidote for the unfortunate effect of the discordant concrete bridge in the purple and gold harmony of the distant Scawfell Crag, where any harshness is veiled in the blue atmospheric depth. A similar, soft effect is to be observed when returning after a day on the fells in the late afternoon, especially on one of those showery days which produce the rich colours peculiar to our climate. By this time the sun is well round in the west. The rocks are freshly wet with rain, and, if one turns on Brown Tongue to look back at the familiar face of the crags, the sunlight will be seen to be reflected brightly from the sheer, smooth wall about the middle. One gleaming patch shines with all the radiance of a silver hatchment. This is the Flake of the Central Buttress. When approached in the morning all the effects assume a grimness in perfect keeping with the notorious defences which this buttress presents against attack.

These towering crags have been the stage whereon have been played a little tragedy, much comedy and a farce. The side entrances are by Mickledore and Lord's Rake. But for the initiated the great rock face between responds to the 'open sesame' of their skill. The ridges leap out into bold relief; the hollows sink back into ever more gloomy recesses. These buttresses and bays resolve themselves into a dozen hidden staircases, all different and all delightful. But, when the last has yielded up its secrets, a sense of loss drives the curious climber to seek out a new way, which shall be worth all the rest. Such is the Central Buttress, towards which I set out about 9 o'clock one August morning (1921), accompanied by Mr Bentley Beetham, of the Fell and Rock Climbing Club.

As we pounded along past the little school, over the footbridge and the clattering stiles, around the foot of Lingmell and up Brown Tongue, we hoped to be the only party bound for Scawfell. It was a fine, warm morning, and the trudge seemed less tedious than usual. We discussed the many hundreds of feet of very fair climbing, up and down, that had been squeezed into the two days' practice necessary to put us into condition. At last when the effort of scrambling up the talus ejected from Lord's Rake put an end to conversation, we stole occasional glimpses at the broad precipice of the Central Buttress, marked off by Moss Ghyll on one side and Botterill's Slab on the other. By the time we had reached the little level patch of gravel at the foot of the Pinnacle Low Man

I was eagerly pointing out the redoubtable Crack. From the lunch place, where we stood, the famous Flake looks very small and distant, whilst the Crack appears hopelessly inaccessible. Seeing that this was our first halt, I felt justified in exercising great deliberation in the act of changing into rubbers, and frequently paused to point out what were, very likely, invisible features of the course. The result was that Beetham was kept waiting while I slowly struggled into a tight jersey. The appearance of a large party topping the mound of Brown Tongue drove us off hurriedly to stake our claim at the foot of the Central Buttress, a few yards east beyond Moss Ghyll.

We were not clear in our minds exactly where the new first pitch began, but familiarity with the regular structure of the rocks forming this precipice convinced us that the subsidiary buttress, which confronted us, could be climbed. Here, as elsewhere on the crag, the divisional joints are roughly at right angles to each other. The altered volcanic ashes weather very conveniently into quadrangular blocks and columnar ribs presenting usually three faces. The two sides are not quite vertical. They tilt slightly to the south and east respectively, and the upper face dips accordingly. On Keswick Brothers' route this causes the repeated westward traverses to present difficulties in the form of ledges sloping the wrong way, and faces which overhang. When the climber faces east, as on the slabs of the Collie Exit of Moss Ghyll, the climbing is much easier if steeper. Every pitch on the Central Buttress bears out the principle that the holds are good or bad according to whether the climber faces east or west. Especially is this the case throughout the first two pitches.

The fact that we had brought along two ropes showed that we had not entered too lightheartedly upon our ambitious enterprise, though I for one should have been at a loss to answer, had I been asked, how I intended to use them. Perhaps the fact that two ropes are stronger than one indicated a fear of catastrophe on the Flake. Now that we had brought the spare length of fifty feet, Beetham volunteered to carry it with us, and we tied on the eighty feet. Starting up a corner between a rib and the main wall, I realised that another factor enters into the consideration of the going besides the quality of the little ledges. Their quantity is a telling factor. The place reminded one of the big adjacent slab. The holds were small, few and far between, and at thirty feet up they failed altogether. A one-step traverse had to be negotiated with great care. The next corner on the left was now occupied and followed without much difficulty. Ledges increased finally into platforms, and when the rope ran out I was able to settle down comfortably upon a grassy bank to admire Beetham's remarkably speedy climbing.

This was very fine, but unfortunately it led us too far to the left. The foot of the Flake now lay off to the right some fifty feet higher. The only means of access was a staircase, whose risers averaged twelve feet, and the treads rather less. The whole system was of course tilted to our disadvantage when attacked from this direction. Moreover, the overflow of the buttress water system maintained a steady supply over the stairway to the obvious satisfaction of succulent lichen, and to the trials due to tilt was added the slipperiness of slime. As usual, the first step was the most trying. To reach it at all, one had to move out and up along dwindling ledges until, when poised over deep space, the sloping top could be reached. Discretion would surely have proved the better part of valour had not a helpful little recess come to hand, which made the squirm upon the jellied surface tolerably safe. Then throwing aside all pretence of style I shuffled on puttees and breeches to the second step. When safely arrived on the landing, I found to my chagrin that Beetham was coming upstairs in a perfectly sober manner, instead of behaving like an inebriated Gulliver after a wet day in Brobdingnag.

The occurrence of a slimy pitch may be expected beneath such a ledge as the one we had now reached. The absorbent loam seems capable of storing up large quantities of moisture, which slowly sipes over the pitch below even after days of dry weather.

This grassy ledge lies about 150 feet above the Rake's Progress, and we could walk about and enjoy the airiness of the situation in comfort. The immense sweep of Botterill's Slab was really impressive. Very fine, too, was Moss Ghyll, teeming with associations dear to climbers. The two pitches, which we had just passed, emphasised the depth and steepness of the downward prospect. Upward, and most impressive of all, soared the vast expanse of the smooth wall of the buttress – and the Flake.

The ledge is called the Oval. It is, as its name implies, bigger than Tennis Court Ledge. It forms part of a terrace which peters out at its extremities, on the east within an exasperatingly short distance of Botterill's Slab, and on the west about as far from the top of the third pitch of Moss Ghyll. It will be remembered that it was discovered by the party who designed the Girdle Traverse. The feature that claimed our attention was the Flake, which springs up in a vertical sweep of seventy feet from the neglected turf of the Oval. The Flake is a thin leaf of rock which the frosts are peeling off the great smooth face of the Buttress, leaving more than a crack but less than a chimney, a fissure too wide for wedging, yet too narrow to enter. The right-hand side of a capital K represents the outline of the margin of the Flake seen in profile. This accords with the rule stated above; the first thirty feet are easy, up and to the left, while the chimney, or crack proper, is all but impossible, up to the right. In the second part, forty feet high, the difficulty is due to the overhang, which becomes pronounced above a chockstone, lodged twelve feet or so from the top. One may search far before one finds a prettier climbing problem than the Flake Crack.

Beetham thought it would go and said so. I did neither. Both ropes were brought into use. The first thirty feet of rock were soon scaled to a ledge nine inches wide. We took the precaution to thread a rope at once. Looking up we saw that two pronounced bulges precede the overhang. I climbed around and stood upon the first, while Beetham squeezed him-

The Crest.

Chief Difficulty.

Chockstone.

THE FLAKE
CRACK,
SCAWFELL.

Second Bulge.

First Bulge.

First Thread.

The Oval.

C.D.F.

115

self as securely as possible into his awkward corner. When he was firm I attacked the second more interesting bulge. Its mildness was a little disappointing, but the next fifteen feet of smooth wall compensated adequately. By the time I had reached two holds, which are destined to be well-known by reason of their rarity, the left one on the edge of the Flake and the right one upon the wall itself, I had begun thoroughly to enjoy myself. The rock was sound and the climbing simple. It is true that it was extremely strenuous going, but it was just as hard work to remain still, and there was always the splendid flat top of the tall, narrow chock to justify any slight 'overdraft' on reserves. As soon as I could, I hitched one rope across the top and dropped my arms to rest. While threading the other rope on the Flake side of the jammed block I found a short, blackened fragment of old rope, firmly wedged. It is still there, its suggestion of mythical legend perhaps accentuated by the harsh croaking of ravens, wheeling over Mickledore.

On Beetham's advice I made loops around my hitch, which could not possibly slip, and sat in them. So comfortable did I feel in this quaint resting place, gripping the chockstone with my knees, that I was tempted to see what I could make of the last ten feet, and must have annoyed Beetham immensely by various very foolish and utterly useless antics on and around the chock, before I came down upon ropes to which the term 'double-double' applied. Then, not being in the least hungry, but greatly nonplussed, we achieved the obvious by adjourning for lunch.

We were not, after all, alone on the crags. Two friends were keenly interested in our doings, because they themselves had designs upon the Flake Crack, and had lugged up a pot-holing life-line, known to many of our members, with the idea of studying the pitch from above. They reached the top of the Flake by way of the summit, and we reported progress, agreeing with their remark that our climbing was yet to begin. They did not accept our suggestion that they should 'come through' us, but queued it up above. I, for one, felt somewhat in the way, and we did not keep them waiting long before returning to the ropes left hanging, one threaded and the other from the hitch.

Little did any of us think that within five minutes the pitch would be successfully, even comfortably, climbed. But so it was, and it may be of interest to describe in detail the novel tactics brought into play to avoid defeat, to which the peculiar flagstone shape of the chock was vital. This time Beetham volunteered to lead as far as the chock. He tied himself on the hitched rope, the slack of which I drew in as he walked quickly up the wall, using both sections of the threaded rope for pulling. At the chock he seated himself in loops of his own rope passed over the rock and tied, and with feet firmly planted on either side of the chockstone, found that his hands could be freed without impairing his security. Then my turn came. At the cost of considerable hemp, but of little effort, I hauled myself up in the manner I have seen adopted by steeplejacks on a church spire, lacking only the counterpoise, the pulley, and the seat, and soon arrived at the rendezvous. Here we went into committee. Beetham invited me to use him as freely as I would any jammed boulder, and I tried to grace my compunction in grating over his frame by calling attention to my rubber shoes. Without more ado Beetham trussed his near side leg with both hands and made a fine stirrup from which I mounted to his equally firm shoulders. It was fortunate my friend was staunch, as he sat dangling in the loops, or our escapade would have been March madness. Both hands were needed to maintain a very unstable balance as I straightened my knees on each side of a steady head. The grip of the hands upon the tapering edges of the Flake was enough to prevent a backward crash, but the sharp, hollowed crest was still out of reach, Beetham offered his head. This improved matters in one direction. Still I craved support for the left foot, which simply would not grip on the smooth wall, and it was promptly impounded and jammed hard. Agitation immediately gave way to complacency. Very carefully, very confidently, the left hand slid up the outside face of the Flake until the fingers curled over and hooked the sharp crest. Then, with feelings unbecoming of expression to a man who has reached my side of middle age, I enjoyed the luxury of lusty hauling, which was sheer joy with such a hold and such space below to spur one's efforts.

The Flake Crack was vanquished for the second time, and the pleasure we derived from the successful accomplishment of our scheme was due as much to the safety of the moves as to any originality of the methods. Stirred by impatience and some curiosity, perhaps, one of our friends was crawling at this moment carefully along the knife-edge of the crest of the Flake, and drew near the end, when we met literally face to face. The situation was ludicrously unexpected, and the exclamation 'They're up!' was accepted as an intimation of surprise, and a quaint form of congratulation. It was only a half-truth, however, Beetham was still playing the part of Prometheus on the face of the crag out of sight below. I hauled in my rope and threw the end down to my partner, so that he could tie on properly. After casting off his moorings from the chock, Beetham found no difficulty in joining me astride the knife-edge.

Pictures of the crest of the Flake, wonderful as they are, hardly do justice to the situation. The sense of height is absent in a photographic impression. The fifty feet of jagged edge, 'so thin as to be perforated in places', are foreshortened disproportionately, and the smooth, inhospitable wall, sweeping upwards into the blue above, does not appear on the print. With a guide's air of appropriation I turned to Beetham – 'What do you think of this for a traverse, Beetham?' Beetham duly appraised the vertical walls and the undulating margin of the crest between – 'Just the place for a hand traverse!' ejaculated the epicure.

I crawled along the edge, and scaled the upward sweep of fifteen feet to a pillar at the far end, before I could look back to pay attention to the rope. There was Beetham approaching calmly upright upon the edge, and with pointed toes and right shoulder against the rock wall – walking, while calmly coiling the spare rope!

We joined Kelly and Bower, and made up a party of four to finish the climb according to the directions on the printed sheet carried by one of them. Our route was now indicated by a huge rift, the Bayonet-shaped Crack. To reach its foot the smooth wall had to be recrossed at higher level by a course roughly parallel to the top of the Flake. A jutting piece of rock marked the place and served as an anchorage. All agreed that the next traverse was 'steep'. For about fifteen feet the climber depends entirely upon his footing, and this is hard to find and keep. At the end across a small gap the Overhanging Buttress must be climbed for another twenty feet, with Hollow Stones peeping up through the window of the Flake Crack between the feet. From the top of the buttress I enjoyed acting the part of spectator in a skilful game played by experts, whose well-known skill was 'all out' upon a traverse, which had the qualities of an 'exceptionally severe', steepness, absence of holds, and exposure, with the edge of the Flake below like the huge, upturned blade of a bill-hook, the sword of Damocles inverted.

Leaving Beetham to bring up the others I turned to admire at close quarters the so-called Crack. This striking feature of Scawfell Crag was obviously named from its aspect from a distance. It is about as big as Walker's Gully, and of more interest to botanists than to climbers. Judging from its steepness it is very unlikely that it would detain either enthusiast long enough to do more than collect a few chance specimens, with which he would descend. The floor has been removed. We preferred the buttress, and rounded the notch, crossed the V Ledge, and arrived at a most fascinating corner.

Some day I hope to return to this pleasantly secluded eyrie and smoke a pipe in the sunshine there. It is at the very top of the lofty grooves on the east of Moss Ghyll, which have been attempted in the less discreet assaults upon the Central Buttress. The view down these will always stir the imagination of a climber. The most disturbing fact is that one looks down to the third pitch of the Ghyll only to plot out a route up again, where every hold is plainly visible, and – how can I describe it? – it only just goes. The nervous strain drives one to shut out the shuddering exposure, and gaze around at the broader, beautiful landscape, tranquil, soft, and restful.

To-day was all hustle and hurry. Once I should have enjoyed the remaining 200 feet of climbing up the west of the Bayonet-shaped Crack, across it at the crook, then up the east side to the summit, and it would still be interesting under conditions of snow and ice. But just now the feeling of regret that the game was ended was somewhat depressing after the buoyancy that had brought one so far. The slope gradually eased off and four hours from the start we unroped on the summit. The time was not long, and there is every hope that on another occasion we may be able to spin it out even more.

Beetham agrees that we never extracted more enjoyment from scrambling anywhere together than we did from our introductory visit to Herford's Buttress. 'It was great, man!' writes Beetham. I hope it will not be considered out of place to express admiration for the work of the enterprising explorers, whose exceptional skill and daring placed at our disposal a course unrivalled in fantastic rock-scenery, in intricate routefinding, and in scope for skilful climbing.

The Yorkshire Ramblers' Club Journal, Vol V, No 15, 1922

Whatever the Fell & Rock thought about the second ascent, they could not pretend that it hadn't happened and, immediately following Holland's panegyric, the FRCC Journal contained an account by Bentley Beetham, Frankland's second on the second successful attempt. The article's position in the Journal is interesting. It is almost as if it was an editorial decision to ensure the reader paid due respect to the first ascent before discovering about the second.

Beetham's article is also strangely muted. For a man who would talk up the scrappiest string of crag-lets as an interesting or entertaining way of spending a day and stoutly defend the virtues of vegetation as a point of aid, his assessment of CB is, to say the least, laconic. It was almost as if he were going through the motions, as one with a minor role in the after-dinner speeches whose job is to thank the appropriate par-ties before introducing the star attraction.

What is not said is more important. Not a word about the progenitors or any comparison between then and now. No sense of personal achievement or satisfaction – he might have been a disinterested observer, hovering alongside Frankland's solo effort.

Certainly, no suggestion that this could be claimed as the first ascent of the climb as a whole. Only when the Flake is passed does the style relax and the jocular tone found in his Borrowdale guide begin to surface.

Perhaps he felt he had betrayed the Fell & Rock by supporting an invader to breach its sanctum sanctorum. Perhaps, like so many others after, he simply found the whole experience awesome.

Scafell Central Buttress

Bentley Beetham, 1921

The Editor has asked me to write something about the Central Buttress – unfortunately, I have nothing to record, except that it is simply magnificent. Probably he, being true to type, will say that this is not quite enough, so I must cast round for something additional to say.

If only the Central Buttress was an orthodox gully one could take it seriatim, pitch by pitch, and so fill up a few lines, but it isn't, and so perhaps I had better confine myself to our own ascent – a personal account, in fact – and leave to another* a detailed description of the climb.

I had hurried back from bad weather and the Alps to join Frankland (YRC) for a few days at Wasdale. Both of us were pretty fit, and we decided to go to feel – no, not to 'look at' it, it isn't wise! – the famous Flake Crack. We took two ropes, a fifty and an eighty. Of course, with Frankland leading, the

* See Mr C D Frankland's article on the Central Buttress in this year's *Yorkshire Ramblers' Club Journal.*

way up to the Oval direct from the Rake scarcely seemed to count; it was taken as if it were part of the route to the climb and nothing more, but in point of fact there is difficulty in this first section.

Arrived at the Oval, we prospected the Crack – a fearsome place enough, but made just reasonable by the presence of two chockstones, behind which a rope can be passed on the ascent. To reach the first of these is nothing: to reach and pass a rope behind the second is everything, the very crux of the whole situation. But it is a desperate struggle; progress can only be made by using an unsatisfying arm wedge, and from here onwards the crack, all too obviously, gets steadily worse. True, temporary respite is afforded immediately above by a large projecting jammed stone, but beyond this the inclination of the overhang increases, while the holds decrease, aye, almost vanish. Frankland made a truly magnificent effort to lead straight through with it. He must have spent more than half an hour struggling in the crack before he had to give it up – what such a struggle means none but those who have been in a similar place for a like time can realise.

The rocks were slightly 'condensation' damp; no hold or grip for the right foot could be found, and on this day, at all events, it simply would not go, so, leaving the ropes threaded and thereby the work more than half achieved, we descended to the foot of Deep Ghyll for lunch.

Within an hour we were back on the Oval again considering the next assault. It was obvious that on the upper section footholds were imperatively needed, in order to counteract the overhang, arms alone could not suffice, and so I suggested that I should go up to the big jammed stone (which projects some eighteen inches), and make myself secure and comfortable there, so that my anchored body might provide the missing holds. With the ropes already 'in situ' this was an easy matter, and in ten minutes the required lump of flesh was dangling like a pendant, free but perfectly secure, immediately beneath the jammed stone. All my limbs were then quite free to form steps wherever wanted, and Frankland came quickly up on the other rope. First he stood upon my left thigh, held horizontally, and braced into a firm strut by both arms, then upon the shoulders, next upon the head, a final step or rather stay being afforded by the upturned palms of both hands. The corner of the horizontal edge of the Flake could now just be reached, and by a strong arm pull he was up in a moment. This upper section of the crack must be very trying to lead. The overhang is quite exceptional – you are hanging some ten–twelve feet out beyond the foot of the crack, and a stance on human flesh (proverbially weak) never feels really secure but of course Frankland found *no* difficulty in it.

The traverse along the edge of the Great Flake is simply wonderful. As regards situation, there is nothing like it in the whole of Lakeland, but it does seem a pity that most of it should be so dead easy, only a walk in fact, or, if the nerves are not too steady, an easy straddled crawl. If twenty feet or so of it *had* to be done as a hand traverse, it would be ideal.

Above the Flake we found Bower and Kelly, who were prospecting downwards; they joined us, and we finished the remainder of the climb together.

We had thought that as soon as the crack had been accomplished, the rest of the climb would present no serious difficulty, but it proved otherwise. Indeed, some of the traversing movements above the Flake are as difficult as anything on the Buttress. Fortunately, these traverses are short, but they are practically holdless, and as sensational as their situation on the upper part of the Scafell face would suggest. They appear to have been designed for a race of climbers having suctorial pads on their digits, like those of a Gecko. Anyhow, one of our party – a lover of the delicate traverse – acknowledged that on one of these 'mauvais pas' his only means of retaining a balance was the nail of one finger, the pads of all the others having slowly slipped; hence it may be inferred that these places are about as steep as is quite safe.

I do not feel that the route we followed above the Flake is the only possible one direct to the top. Next year we intend to take a camera and to poke about the climb in a leisurely manner, and so get a truer impression of its parts, the relative difficulties of which may then seem changed – at any rate we hope to get some photographs to do justice to this splendid piece of rock.

FRCC Journal, Vol V, No 3, 1921

A third ascent took place in 1923. It was a strong party led by A S Pigott, the first climber to open up the main cliffs of Clogywn Du'r Arddu. He was supported by Morley Wood who, as George Bower once remarked, 'was quite willing to follow Fred Pigott to Hell, ready to shoulder him across the Styx if need be.'* The climb was apparently not written up. As the FRCC Journal lamented: 'It would be interesting to hear the impressions on the Flake of Mr Pigott, who led the third and only other ascent of this climb, but unhappily the Editor of the Rucksack Club has failed to enforce disciplinary measures.'

There was still no sign of a successful attempt by Kelly, despite the obvious interest noted by Beetham and Frankland. It is clear that, even a decade after it was first climbed, only the strongest were considering the possibility and that once done was enough for any man. It is therefore surprising that the next party consisted of a repeater and a woman.

In the article that follows, Mabel Barker describes her ascent with C D Frankland. She was only the fourth person to lead the top, and most intimidating,

*High Peak, Byne & Sutton, 1966.

section of the Flake and, despite the modesty of her account, was probably the first to lead it unaided. Whereas her male predecessors had had their feet supported by outstretched arms, Barker climbed the crack unassisted. There was the inevitable male outcry at Frankland's irresponsibility in allowing such a possibility to occur, but the facts indicate that this was mere prejudice rather than sound judgement.

As Barker's account makes clear, she and Frankland had been at pains to ensure they were up to the task. The previous year they had completed the Girdle Traverse of Scafell in a very fast time (which, by definition, must have meant that Barker was more than competent to lead at a high standard) and, before the attempt on CB, they had returned from a fortnight in Skye 'splendidly fit'. The weather had been excellent and the rock, by the time they started their ascent, was in good condition.

The condescension was directed less at Barker in particular than at women climbers in general. Dorothy Pilley recalls 'hard stares from the women and sniggers from the louts' when she appeared in public in climbing gear and, on another occasion, being ordered by the manageress of the Sligachan Hotel to change into a skirt for dinner. The Journal of the

Pinnacle Club contains many examples of the lengths women had to go to disguise their recreational habit from parents and friends. These included clandestinely changing out of church-wear into trousers and, *in extremis*, disguising the true holiday location by arranging for friends to despatch pre-written postcards from more suitable resorts.

Perhaps the male climbing world should not have been so surprised. Pilley had always maintained that when it came to balance climbing, women, with their lower centre of gravity, had an advantage over men. Barker's performance on the Flake suggested that if a route depended on the type of muscular application that was closer to the dynamic movement of the gymnast than the heaving of the weightlifter, then women might be equally well equipped to deal with the advances that rock climbing was making. Current performances have proved that this supposition had more than a sound basis.

Or perhaps the outcry sprang from a different base. In some quarters, it may have been difficult to accept that a rambler from Yorkshire had been the first to climb every part of the Flake in every possible combination. In another, the unwillingness to face up to the truth that the real reason why no locals had made a series of further ascents was because, as Ashley Abraham suggested when he first put the cat among the pigeons, they really weren't up to it.

On Scawfell

Mabel Barker, 1925

August, 1924, was a wet month, almost as wet as August, 1923, but once again we spent it in camp at Seathwaite. My camping comrades, who had narrowly escaped drowning by the swollen Derwent, and squashing by a falling tree, insisted upon returning there and nowhere else. One of them was on honeymoon, and wanted to ensure a thorough initiation for her husband, and so had to have her way; and perhaps I didn't take much persuading, anyway. But more than chaff for their love of water, or congratulation on their grit are due to my cheery fellow campers, for whatever happens to them, it is I who am sure to get all the best going out of camping in Borrowdale.

That August, 1924, for example, while we sat at the foot of the swollen Sour Milk Ghyll, C D Frankland came and stayed at Seathwaite Farm for a week. That week was fine, all except one day, on which we stayed in camp to receive all his families, none of whom turned up; but all mine did. It simply poured.

I believe they think I arranged it on purpose!

He suggested one day, rather casually, that we should go and do the Girdle Traverse on Scawfell. I was thrilled at the idea, but somewhat dubious of bringing it off. All I knew of it then was that it was reputed to take about six hours, and included Botterill's Slab (which had been pointed out to me as 'a foul place'!) However, I had never climbed till I had had enough, and the chance of so long on the rocks!

'Which end shall we begin?' said I innocently, as we wandered through Hollow Stones.

'O, the Mickledore end, I think,' said my partner. I did not know that this was not the usual proceeding, and that it was even doubtful if a complete reversal had ever been made. We were nearer it, and it was convenient for the lunch pool on Mickledore, and chimed with my own inclinations.

Not having done all of the Girdle Traverse the usual way, I can offer no very definite opinion as to respective merits and difficulties, but one thing is obvious. Taking it our way, the descent of Botterill's Slab comes almost at once, very early in the climb and before one has 'got going'. It has to be tackled in cold blood, and it remains a vivid memory of one of the thinnest bits of climbing I ever did. No muscular effort is required, nor any particularly long reach, so it is theoretically possible for anyone – and just possible. The upper part, where it is climbed on the edge, is not so bad; but these holds fade away, and one has to traverse on to the face of the slab. Here I have the impression of a long, long pause. In retrospect I seem to stand for the greater part of the afternoon on the ample security of a half inch ledge, wishing I had brought a pocket lens with which to look for a handhold; assured by my optimistic partner that there was a foothold somewhere beneath me; wondering if suction could be applied to the rock. Reluctantly, I had just said that I didn't see what to do with it, but come on the rope, when I tried something – have no idea what – and with immense astonishment and relief found my right foot in the hold. The rest was easy; but CDF's descent of that slab as watched from the belay at the foot of it was probably one of the most beautiful bits of balance climbing ever seen.

After that it was mostly pure joy. I am a poor hand at writing up a climb, for I fail to remember detail, and when asked how I liked so and so, am generally driven to reply vaguely that I suppose it went, while trying in vain to remember what my questioner is talking about, and being at the same time seized with a horrible suspicion that I never really did that climb at all, but got off it on to some alternative and far inferior route. If a description is available I then read it to see what we are supposed to have done. The result is unconvincing, and I am inexorably driven to the conclusion that I haven't done a single decent climb in the Lake District! Or would be, but that there are such vivid and purple moments. One cannot very well get 'off the climb' on Botterill's Slab or the Flake Crack!

Anyway, I did read up the previous accounts of the Girdle Traverse, and the Guide (when it came) with great interest, and must surely have missed out large portions of that climb. (And as this is being written by the Mediterranean, I cannot get them up again now.) But I remember the traverse from the Fives Court very clearly, for it went well that day; and the thrill of reaching Hopkinson's Cairn for the first time, and looking from it into Deep Ghyll, is unforgettable.

It began to rain slightly while we were on the Pinnacle Wall above Deep Ghyll, and my partner betrayed some anxiety, and hurried a little. Now I thought that the Traverse continued round the West

Wall (and why not?), and when asked the time, replied tranquilly that it was 4.20 (we had started from Mickledore at 2.00 precisely). 'Hasn't your watch stopped?' said he. 'Good heavens, we'll be on the top of the Pinnacle in ten minutes!' We were. I believe he would have suggested the Central Buttress then and there but for the rain; also we wanted to go to Wasdale to vindicate the character of my blameless watch.*

So when on August 17th of this year we returned from a fortnight in Skye, splendidly fit and in beautiful weather, we suggested to the camp in general that we might as well go to Scawfell next day; the Corridor Route always made a good expedition, and some new friends had joined us who were anxious to see some climbing. The day was fine, and we set off in a leisurely mood, which persisted through lunch in Hollow Stones. But this late start was partly a strategic move in order to give the rocks time to dry (for the morning had been misty) and about 2 o'clock we went right on to the climb.

The first ascent of the Central Buttress of Scawfell was made in 1914 by S W Herford and G S Sansom,

* Herford had suggested that 'a party familiar with the route could finish it in six to seven hours'. (Ed)

C F Holland, C G Crawford and D G Murray, and having been pronounced 'unjustifiable' was again climbed in 1921 by C D Frankland and B Beetham. A third ascent was made in 1923 by A S Pigott, Morley Wood, and J B Meldrum; so ours was the fourth ascent and Frankland is thus the only man who has been up it twice. It was this, of course, which made it possible for us to climb it as we did, straight through without loss of time or undue expenditure of energy, and with very great enjoyment.

The rocks were dry, but not in perfect condition according to CDF, because of the amount of lichen which has grown on them since his last visit; but I cannot blame the lichen for the fact that during the first part of the climb I felt decidedly scared. No doubt I would have climbed better and more confidently had we done something rather more modest by way of prelude, for most of us probably take a little time to get warmed up, and this was again like meeting Botterill's Slab early in the Traverse; but my nervousness was partly due to respect for the climb. It seemed a sort of impertinence to approach the Flake Crack at all – and I had dreamed of it for a year!

Up the rib on to the Oval was just good stiff face

climbing with small holds which did not always appear when one first called for them. CDF seemed to walk up lightly with a jest about their insufficiency, and I crawled after, endorsing it heartily.

We had only an eighty-foot rope (which proved ample) and he ran out most of it on this section. When I joined him near the foot of the Flake he seemed wrapped in meditation. There was the question of that wretched thread belay. We both knew it wouldn't be wanted, but of course it had to go on. He got up a short pitch, and I came right along to the foot of the Crack, where there is a good enough stance, narrow but quite sufficient. The left hand and arm can go right into the crack, but there is nothing to hold there, and there is nothing for the right hand. It is a position where the second can wait comfortably for any length of time in reason, but cannot safeguard the party. If the leader came off during the difficult business of climbing up to the chockstone and putting the loops of rope over it the second could not possibly save either of them. We therefore wasted – no, spent – about twenty minutes of precious time and temper, he trying to induce a loop of rope to pass behind a small chockstone near him, while I tried to see it, and then to catch it with the left hand and pull it through. Coils of rope seemed to be fed into the crack, while nothing happened so far as I could see! At last it appeared; I pulled it through and put my left arm through it. Meanwhile, however, there was time to examine the crack near me and I think that there is a small chockstone, far in and pretty low down, which might serve for a belay if it can be reached and if a rope will go round it. If so, it would be a great simplification and help at this part of the climb.

The loop belay settled, however, CDF led up the crack, and passed three loops over the chockstone and under himself. I pulled on each loop to his direction, but not quite to his satisfaction, for the rope sagged a little, and he said the loops were lower than on his former ascent. He then called to me to come up as quickly as I could. I did so, but by this time was too excited to climb decently, and scrambled up in an untidy fashion, remarking as I arrived that I was tired. It was a thoroughly commonplace observation, meaning nothing, but was bad psychology, for I fear it alarmed my partner. But after the long wait and this short struggle, the next few moments of tense excitement and rapid action passed quickly, and I do not really know what happened; except that I got on to and over my partner and off his head as quickly as possible. He says he felt for my foot to hold it if necessary, but could not find it, and I do not know where it went. Probably, being slimmer than former climbers, I got farther into the crack, and chimneyed it. I faced out, and think there was a small hold far up on the inside wall. Almost at once I felt the top of the Flake with the left hand. 'I've got it!' I said, thrilled with the realisation that the thing was virtually done, and there probably was not a happier woman living at that moment!

There is a good belay a few feet along the Flake. I pulled in the slack as the loops were taken off the chockstone, and CDF came up very quickly on a tight rope. We looked at the traverse in front of us. It is a marvellous situation, and it is difficult now to believe that I have been there.

'Beetham walked along that and coiled the rope,' said CDF. 'Well, I'm going to walk along it,' I said, and did so, but with the utmost caution, and with both hands on the wall; and then saw to it that as CDF followed there wasn't any loose rope for him to coil! Another upright piece of Flake follows ('dead easy') and another broader edge, still to the left and leading into a collection of broken rocks easily visible from below. Here CDF took the lead again, and just then we heard voices and came within sight of two men on Keswick Brothers, who asked with some interest what we were on.

'Central Buttress: just got up the Flake,' said my partner with careful indifference and just as his second appeared. There are moments when it is rather good fun to be a woman. Probably no lady in history was ever so sure of creating a mild sensation by the mere fact of being where she was.

The traverses to the right again, and especially the second one, are undoubtedly very thin indeed. Its poor handholds and sloping footholds are just about the limit. There is nothing to put one's weight on, and the only method is a slow and careful change of balance. Nor must the climber take any risk of a slip, for though the stances are good, the belays are poor. The climb is by no means over when the famous Flake is conquered.

But after the second traverse it is relatively easy, and my memory of its detail is vague.

There was a nice slabby wall presenting no special difficulty, and the climb finishes among several small slabs where I lost my partner's trail, so that we chose different ones. We forgot to look at the time, but our patient support party watching from Hollow Stones, say it was just two and a half hours till they saw us on the sky line, and we joined them again in three hours exactly, having come down Moss Ghyll (without help from Professor Collie, as we think, but is there only one Step?)

I was told later that there had been some criticism and talk of risk taken on this climb, and I would like to say here that no risk whatever was taken by either climber. All the rules of the game were most carefully and conscientiously observed, and had there been any risk at any moment I should surely know it. I can also say quite honestly that at no point did I find myself having any serious difficulty with the climbing. Whatever he may say about it, I know very well who was the real leader at every point. Frankland found the route, carried through the difficult matter of engineering the loops over the chockstone, gave calm and clear directions, and took all responsibility. What remained for me was a very real sense of co-operation (absent in some measure from the stiffest slabs and traverses which can be done alone, for I do not think that the Flake Crack is possible for the safest solo climber), and a perfectly splendid climb throughout, compelling respect for it, and giving no excuse for carelessness or relaxed attention at any point. Yet nowhere was there much call upon my very small reserve of muscular strength, nor had I ever the feeling that my power was taxed to the uttermost, and the pitch unjustifiable without the moral support of the rope.

FRCC Journal, Vol VII, No 1, 1925

But one challenge remained and that was to climb the Flake from bottom to top without the physical or moral support of a second suspended on the chockstone. Frankland had considered it possible (technically it was a similar standard to Green Crack, his showpiece on Almscliff) but his failure must have acted more as a deterrent than an incentive to those who followed. The problem lay with the technical nature of the climbing. Unless the climber was built on the sylph-like lines of Mabel Barker, there seemed little alternative but to layback the full length of the overhanging section. The consequence of strength in the arms evaporating or a foot slipping would be likely to have been disastrous.

The general feeling about this particular gymnastic manoeuvre is perhaps best summed up by the guidebook description of the third pitch of B Route on Gimmer. It reads: 'Amen Corner. Ten feet. Layback the obvious crack.' It is unusual for a pitch to have a name of its own and, when it does, it is generally prosaically descriptive (The Hand Traverse) or attributive (Gibson's Chimney). But in this case, the gallows humour, usually reserved for defining a particularly nasty climb as a whole, is applied to a part. The guidebook instruction indicates the course of action; the nomenclature the potential outcome.

But Amen Corner is at least two grades easier than the Flake, in a relatively unexposed position and about a third of the length. Something a little more than a wing and a prayer was needed if the central buttress of Scafell was to be climbed free. When it happened, it was, in the history of CB, perhaps the most curious chapter of all. In 1931, Menlove Edwards, with fellow Liverpudlians Bill Stallybrass and Marco Pallis, set off to attempt the route. Jim Perrin, in his extensive and excellent biography of Edwards,* gives an account of how the second saw the events that led up to the climb. Stallybrass caught up with Edwards and Pallis in Hollow Stones to find another party already on the climb. Alf Bridge was engaged on the Flake when his foot slipped and it was only by an act of prodigious strength that he managed to hang on. Shaken, he continued to the chockstone, where he lashed himself in the accepted fashion and whence his party completed the ascent with the standard amount of assistance.

Menlove's party, no doubt a little startled by what

*Menlove, Jim Perrin, Gollancz, 1985.

it had just witnessed, followed. Edwards reached the chockstone and proceeded to bring his second up to him. At this point matters get rather confused. Stallybrass recalls:

> *The whole performance was hair-raisingly chaotic. For some reason I was still carrying the spare line. I gripped hold of Menlove's shoulders and we both swung out from the rock. He seemed to be only very loosely tied on. My strength was by then running out. I seized hold of a spare rope that Menlove had secured to the chockstone and lowered myself until I could jam my body in the crack and take a rest. Menlove meanwhile was making fresh arrangements with the rope. Suddenly he called out: 'I'm going to have a go!' Next moment he was laybacking up the crack, unbelayed, and was soon at the top.*

But what was really significant was the fact that Edwards later confessed to Stallybrass that he had always intended to climb the Flake unaided, but 'had felt obliged at least of making a show of giving me a chance to climb over him in the orthodox manner'. Circumstantial evidence suggests that this had indeed been his intention and the hair-raising chaos was deliberately contrived to prevent the second from succeeding. He had been working out in a gymnasium beneath the Adelphi Hotel to strengthen the muscles particularly applicable to laybacking and, that summer, had been the first person to solo the Flake Crack at Helsby, a fifty-foot layback with the crux at the very top.

But the point of real interest is why Edwards hid his real intentions. He was no great upholder of orthodoxy, either on or off the rock. Yet somehow he, too, was caught up in the myth that the climb deserved unique respect. Kirkus, in a letter of congratulation, was less reverential: 'To do it straight off without exploration was a marvellous feat. Three cheers for the Climbers' Club.'*

This was an early sign that the standard of Welsh climbing had surpassed that of the Lakes and there is no doubt that Herford would have been the first to applaud. As, indeed, he would have been delighted with the next twin accounts of the first descent. After all, this neatly completed a naphand of climbing of the most famous section of rock in the district.

*Menlove, Jim Perrin, Gollancz, 1985.

From Both Ends of the Rope*

M M Barker and J Carswell, 1936-7

M M Barker: Climbing Down

'We don't climb down often enough.' This remark may be true in more than one sense, and certainly it applies to our treatment of most of the more severe routes in Lakeland. We go up them, and come down by some easier way, neglecting in consequence the technique of descending. This seems a pity and means that one maxim of a great climber – never to make a move which cannot be reversed – is often neglected.

As a result of discussion round this point the idea was born of descending the Central Buttress of Scafell. Jack Carswell suggested it – at first tentatively, for it sounded rather crazy; then hopefully as the details were thought out. The main difficulty, the Great Flake itself, could at a pinch be roped down. (I believe this has been done before?) Apart from that, the most severe pitches of the climb are generally

---

*Descriptions by the first man [sic] and the last man on the rope on the occasion of the First Descent of the Central Buttress of Scafell.

admitted to be the traverses: and why should they not go just as well from right to left as from left to right? Nobody had ever tried them that way; they might even be easier.

Therefore I was not too much surprised when on an evening in June, Jack Carswell and Ieuan M B Mendus arrived at Friar Row proposing that we try it next Sunday.

We duly met at Seathwaite, but we did not descend CB. We went up one pitch of Gillercombe Buttress, got soaked to the skin, went home, and spent the rest of the day drying ourselves and our clothes.

But the following Sunday, June 21st, was perfect. We wandered slowly up the Corridor Route: left our spare gear in Hollow Stones, and went up Broad Stand, feeling rather like conspirators. This feeling was heightened by meeting with friends on the top to whom we talked evasively. Having got rid of them, we hunted nervously for the top pitch of Central Buttress, and perhaps our excitement was responsible for the difficulty we had in locating it. But once found, we spent no time in contemplation, but got over the edge as quickly as possible.

Jack Carswell, the originator and leader of the enterprise, naturally came last: but one advantage of climbing down is the increased responsibility at the other end of the rope. The first down has certainly more of the job in hand than the third up: and being in that position I had all the fun of working out the route backwards. To begin with, I went down the first (14th) pitch rather too far left: met wet and rotten rock, and a foothold came off. 'Nice sort of a start,' I thought: but could of course warn the others against repeating my error.

When Ieuan joined me at the belay in the Bayonet-shaped Crack there came what proved to be, for me at least, the most difficult part of the whole climb. The route (Pitch 13) lies down part of the Moss Ghyll Grooves to a small but good stance with no belay. This has to be left for the first traverse and no belay is available till the V Ledge. It looked, and was, extremely thin and exposed, but went delightfully, the rope being eventually carried over a small bracket visible on the skyline from the MGG stance. But the footholds by which this is reached when ascending to it from the V Ledge are well underneath, and cannot be seen from above. I looked at the thing almost too long, for I began to be afraid that it would take more nerve than I possessed to hang on the bracket by my arms alone, in faith that an invisible foothold would materialise. Moreover, I was then so far from the belay in the Bayonet-shaped Crack that Jack and Ieuan could not hear me. I could not even, for some time, get them to give me enough rope for the next move (which would have to be made soon if I was not to fall off from sheer fright!) At last I managed to 'get over' a suggestion that Jack should come to the belay, and then hold Ieuan on the MGG stance, whence my rope would be horizontal and well supported by the bracket (which is no use as a belay, but is slightly hooked, and a rope so held *might* stay on it if a climber came off here). This move was carried out, and I then slipped over on to the V Ledge, finding as usual that 'the difficulties are purely mental.' Ieuan then followed easily, taking my word for it that there were footholds: and I suppose Jack made nothing of it, for I heard no comments from him.

The vertical crack from the V Ledge to the second traverse (11th pitch) looks horrid from above, but its bark is worse than its bite. The traverse also really does go more easily, I think, from right to left: perhaps because one is making for such an obvious and comforting belay. The third traverse (10th pitch) also went beautifully and was a pure joy. We were making good time, and everything in the garden was lovely. But when we all assembled round the Cannon we became aware of an obstacle to our triumphal progress. There was a party coming up!

We arranged ourselves in a prostrate row on Jeffcoat's Ledge, and spent the next hour and a half as pleasantly and patiently as might be. We could not see much of ATH and his party, but could hear quite well, so the wait was not monotonous, and pleasantries were being exchanged long before Ruth appeared and traversed over our recumbent bodies to the belay beyond them. With subsequent members of the party of four (led by S Cross), we traded chocolate for cigarettes, for both Ieuan and I left ours in Hollow Stones, expecting to rejoin them sooner or later – but had not thought it would be so *much* later; and our self-denying ordnance was dissipated in smoke.

When the last foot of the ascending ropes had passed over us we prepared for business.

So far Ieuan, as middle man on the traverses and carrying a spare rope, had had the least interesting time perhaps, but this was a very co-operative affair, and now his turn came. Our order was changed: Ieuan went first along the Flake, Jack next, and I waited at the far end. Ieuan disappeared, belayed by Jack, and after much wangling with ropes announced with what breath was left to him that he had reached the chockstone, and had climbed all the way down. It took some time, and much discussion between the men for him to get the ropes round the chock and himself arranged to their complete satisfaction – (these details I leave to my partner to explain more lucidly than I can) – but when all was ready I passed Jack on the outside of the Flake, and with all the cold-bath thrill that one can get in such a moment, climbed down after Ieuan. We all three climbed this quite clean, without coming on the ropes at all: but when on Ieuan's shoulder, my right foot (I being quite unable to see where it was going) went on and on for a long time into space with no bottom to it. Eventually it found a foothold in what proved to be the poor lad's stomach! So it had to be got out again, with some agony to both, and carried round behind instead. At last, to his great relief, that feat was accomplished, and I went right down to the Oval. That descent is extremely thin, but naturally not so exhausting as an ascent, and one found oneself at the bulge (Pitch 4) with a sort of incredulous relief. The end of the spare rope was thrown down to me, its other end going through the loop on the chockstone and up to Jack. He then climbed down clean (leaving no loop behind on the Flake), over Mendus and down to the bulge, belayed by me. At the bulge he waited while Ieuan untied the loops, save one detached loop over the chock in which he stood and which finally carried the running belay by which Ieuan descended, passed Jack, and joined me on the Oval. Jack then flicked off this remaining loop, and came down to us, leaving no trace of rope behind.

The rest of the descent we were now in the mood to treat as a joke: but in fact it needed care. Our original order was resumed, and I found time at the bottom of Pitch 3 to retrieve some garments lost by the other party. (While on the Oval we could see bits of them on the upper traverses – a foot, or the flick of a rope now and then – and realised how far these traverses overhang the Flake itself.)

Above the last pitch we all met once more. Jack said it went straight down. I said it didn't, and I wouldn't; and after a glance over he agreed cordially. Actually Pitch 1 comes up a good way to the right of the stance we arrived on. It was amusing that our only hesitations over route were with the top and bottom pitches!

Well, it was a great climb!

While walking up that agreeable valley which lies behind Melbreak where my companion was wont to fritter away valuable climbing hours in attempting to obtain photographs of some very refractory buzzards, our conversation turned, as it always does, to climbing.

A joking allusion to CB as a descent deposited the germ of an idea which rapidly attained maturity as the problem was examined. After all, the major difficulties were concentrated in the Flake and the traverses, and why should a traverse be any more difficult from one end than the other? The Flake however, was not to be disposed of so easily, for the purist in me said that it must be climbed, while conscience, with a strong backing of common sense, said I should have recourse to the obvious method and rope down, and the two waged a continuous war up to the very time when we were congregated on the tip of the Flake.

Soon the project developed into a conspiracy with all the secretiveness essential to a good conspiracy. The idea had met with enthusiastic though not unjudicial support from Ieuan M B Mendus who was to be our second, and together we broke the news to Mabel M Barker. Her reply was never in doubt, and we gathered that all her various inchoate engagements were to remain inchoate until the deed was done. Thereafter, it was a standing engagement for every Sunday.

The first attempt was a literal 'wash-out.' We met at Seathwaite and had Ieuan and I been left to ourselves we would have had the wit not to leave the valley, but Mabel who never lets 'I dare not wait upon I would' silently shamed us into climbing the first pitch of Gillercombe Buttress. Whereupon we beat a judicious retreat facilitated by torrents of water after a classical wetting. The famed hospitality of Friar Row boasts many things but male attire is not amongst them, and later that day, draped in two blankets apiece, Ieuan insisted that either he had forgotten how to don a toga or the Romans were only precariously decent. True, we achieved a certain dignity but it was a dignity that could be maintained only in repose.

The next week-end was glorious and after a delightful Saturday at Caldbeck and on Carrock Fell, Mabel Barker, Mendus and myself toiled up from Seathwaite under a broiling sun with a strong torrid east wind which occasioned some slight misgivings at first till we realised that owing to the tilt of the strata we should be fairly sheltered from any wind from the Mickledore end, as proved to be the case.

The problem of whether or not to bathe in Sty-head Tarn, occupied as all discussions on hot days do, just sufficient time for us to get cooled down, a rather lengthy process. The corridor was just as long and dry as ever and it was in a very limp condition indeed that we eventually arrived in Hollow Stones.

We ate a very dry lunch, and after skilfully avoiding a direct question as to our intentions we found the top of the climb, a matter of no small difficulty, and one after the other dropped over the edge.

The downward view from the first few feet of the top pitch (which was unexpectedly awkward) must be unique in Lakeland, and with a wind that made conversation difficult I reflected to myself that we were asking too much, though we could at least have a good day's climbing. The third and second had no difficulty with Pitch 13, but on the next pitch which leads down to the V Ledge and in its upper portions is common to Moss Ghyll Grooves, our difficulties commenced. Comfortably sheltered at the bottom of the top pitch I listened absently to the full-throated but fruitless efforts of Ieuan and Mabel, who were spaced out below me at intervals of forty feet, to establish contact in the teeth of the strong wind; both were audible to me and I finally gathered that she wanted him to descend until he was level with her, the better to receive her instructions with regard to her rope. It transpired that Mabel was standing at the V Ledge end of the traverse (Pitch 12), so while she held to the rock – there being no belay – I joined my second and changing belays with him, let him take up the desired position. He was then able to give her a running belay over the hook on the traverse, after which she descended to the V Ledge.

This awkward operation reinforced the opinion I had formed at the commencement, and I received warnings as to the difficulty. Thus I was cheered to find the traverse one of the most delectable things I have done, and my second said that he was more than relieved when I appeared with a broad smile on my face. But I found the warnings as to the descent on to the V Ledge fully justified. The advice to lower myself, suspended on my hands only, to an invisible foothold was scarcely comforting, but I found it sound.

Foregathered on the V Ledge my friends told me that Sidney Cross, A T Hargreaves and others were ascending the climb. Various suggestions were made as to how to dispose of them, none of which would have met with their approval.

Mabel tripped merrily down the right-angled corner and across the traverse to the pinnacle with only the suggestion of a pause on the traverse itself. However, she advised me to have a doubled rope for the corner but the knowledge imparted by two ascents discounted this.

After slinging a sixty-foot coil over, Ieuan followed in great style. The holds found are not quite as good as one would like – they rarely are – but we were soon on Jeffcoat's Ledge, where we heard voices.

After much precarious craning of necks we discovered that the other party had already reached the Oval, so, not wishing for an audience while manoeuvring at the chockstone, we settled ourselves down for a lengthy wait, and made ourselves more thirsty than ever with chocolate and huge chunks of home-made marzipan (a well-known Friar Row delicacy).

Now commenced a diplomatic exchange which would not have disgraced a Foreign Secretary, the outcome of which, to the dismay of my companions, was the discovery that there were no cigarettes in the party. Thereupon the arrival of the others was more eagerly awaited than ever.

Many were the climbs done and places visited during the ensuing hour, but immediately a smiling face graced the tip of the Flake an agonized duet rang out saying in effect, 'A cigarette, a cigarette, my belay for a cigarette,' which in view of the fact that there were four in the other party might not have been a bad bargain.

The difficulty, or apparent impossibility of accommodating seven people on Jeffcoat's Ledge will be obvious to anyone who has been there, but we did it. The problem of the passage was solved without ceremony in the only possible way, i.e. by their walking over our prostrate bodies and the barbarians actually seemed to enjoy the process. After we had got our respective ropes well tangled they passed on and left us to it.

We changed our order, Ieuan going first, myself second and Mabel last, and leaving her on Jeffcoat's we two edged along the crest of the Flake. The arrangement between us was that Ieuan should climb down to the chockstone and report on whether it was climbable. He lowered himself over the ledge, his hand disappeared; a moment's silence and then a voice gently suggested that I might hold the rope a little tighter if it wouldn't inconvenience me. This, however, was not in accordance with my part of the plan and the rope remained slack, until a voice triumphantly and with not a little surprise announced that its owner had climbed it clean.

It was here that the sixty-foot rope, hitherto Nobody's Darling, came into its own. First, while held by me, Ieuan hooked a short loop of line over the convenient spike below the chockstone and stood in it under the very mistaken impression that it would relieve me of some of his weight. Next he started to tie on to the chockstone, but stoutly denied the existence of a thread. Dialectics ('testing of truth by discussion, logical disputation') even from a lawyer meant nothing to me. I had used the thread twice, and eventually it was found. It is said that mild-mannered, inoffensive people are known to swear on occasion; my second evidently thought this an occasion.

Ieuan, having untied the rope on which he descended, Mabel went down on two ropes, thus disposing of a temporary surplus length. When she was safely on the Oval one length of rope was thrown down to her and the other hauled up by Ieuan, who threaded it through a loop and returned it to Mabel so that she might belay me from below.

I had been perched on the Flake for so long that I

was stiff and sore, so I took a short rest before commencing the descent. This I found less trying than the ascent, because by getting the right shoulder in the Crack one can use sundry small holds on the inside, sufficient to control a descent but not of much help when overcoming the excessive friction of an ascent. Once past the chockstone my rope naturally became a doubled one, and I doubt whether it would be wise to attempt to descend this wall without such a safeguard.

I stopped at the bottom chockstone and once more the second pulled up an end of my rope after Mabel had untied, undid my running thread and rethreaded the rope, this time through the loop in which he was standing, and cast off the loops from the chockstone and descended on the now doubled rope. I was then able to flick off the loop on the spike and join the others on the Oval, leaving no trace of our passage.

We coiled the sixty-foot rope and unceremoniously threw it down to the screes, following later in a much more leisurely fashion. After the mixture of styles above we did not find any trouble with the remaining pitches. The climb, however, maintained its interest until the end, since the bottom pitch is always a pretty problem, and as Ieuan and I stepped off the last foothold we were greeted by Mabel in appropriately feminine manner.

On looking back we agreed that in the previous five and a half hours we had savoured the essence of climbing to the full, and that CB had no rival. As to difficulty we formed the opinion that for those who know the climb there is not much to choose between an ascent or a descent providing the party has some experience in descents. The Flake itself is both easier and safer.

Ieuan and I were proud to have had the company of Mabel Barker. We had read her account of her ascent with Frankland in 1925 many times before we had the pleasure of meeting her. She was the first woman up the climb and it was only appropriate she should also be the first down it.

As we sat in Mrs Edmondson's at midnight that night quaffing tea, Mabel said to us, 'Only one thing remains for you boys.'

'Yes?' we replied.

'To repeat the climb when you are in your 51st year.'

Truly a chastening thought.

FRCC Journal, Vol XI, Nos 30-31, 1936-7

As this particular descent simultaneously covered all remaining corners (other than a solo ascent by a man carrying his dog while reciting suitable extracts from the Lyrical Ballads) that seemed to be that. It is true that Menlove Edwards went on to climb it in hobnailed boots, but that was more a case of fighting inner demons than pushing back the frontiers of rock technique. The Fell & Rockers bravely defended CB's position as the foremost climb in Britain, but in terms of difficulty it was sliding down the scale. Although, dutifully, the new routes on the East Buttress were placed below CB in the Classified List, it was only a question of time before someone examined the cut of the Emperor's jib.

In 1933, A B Hargreaves did just that. Invited by the editor of the FRCC Journal to write an article on climbing in North Wales, he approached the task with some weft. Using CB as a yardstick, he sought to evaluate the relative difficulties of climbing in Cumbria and the Principality. On the evidence of several ascents of each, he deemed the Central Buttress of Scafell to be somewhat easier than Piggot's Climb on Clogwyn Du'r Arddu and the latter to be of a lower order of difficulty than the routes currently being pioneered by Colin Kirkus with a little help from his friends. Moreover, he criticised the majority of the Lakes routes as being not only artificial (he just stopped short of calling them outcrops) but also lacking the challenge traditionally associated with real mountaineering. In fact, he went so far as to state that when visiting in the Lake District, 'one is inclined to be bored with climbs, the only reason for falling off which, would be just letting go.'

Although there was no specific attack on CB, it was there by implication. As the climb could be abandoned at a number of points for easier ground, it was essentially artificial; the crux could be examined on a rope and, when compared with climbs on Cloggy, was not that especially difficult or adventuresome. In fact, it was typical of many of the new hard climbs in the district. Hargreaves cites Gimmer Crack, Hiatus and Route 1 on Pillar as routes spoilt by the facility of easier alternatives. The response from the Fell & Rock in the following year's Journal was a deafening silence and it was not until 1935 that C J Astley Cooper tentatively commented on Hargreaves' 'Welsh Wiles'. This account was more playful than informed and the main point for the defence was the suggestion that 'letting go' in Snowdonia was made all the more difficult because of the tenacious nature of Welsh grass.

By the time the 1956 FRCC guide appeared, the route had been straightened somewhat by a direct start and finish and the historical section had to admit that the developments on the East Buttress (ironically initiated by Kirkus) forced 'even the Central Buttress [...] to bend the knee as far as technical difficulty is concerned'. But, loyal to the last, the Club pronounced that 'as an expedition [it] will probably always hold its place as the finest of all the district has in its gift.' Although it remained on most climbers' list of Routes I Must Do, it started to achieve the status of an elderly relative – someone who is a delight to visit, provided he or she is having a good day. If not yet 'An Easy Day for a Lady', it had begun the slide down the old Alpine scale that ranged from the 'Inaccessible' to that particular abyss of patronising disdain.

There was another public airing in 1986, when the Fell & Rock published a special edition of the Journal to celebrate the centenary of the ascent of its totem pole. In addition to the Needle, due homage was paid to CB with a reprint of Sansom's original account. As a counterpoint, the editor invited Bill

Birkett, an outstanding young climber with many first ascents to his name, to climb Central Buttress and report back. Birkett, who had been 'saving the route for [his] old age', set off in the frame of mind that people adopt when constructing obituaries for those about to depart. To add authenticity to the venture, his second was 62 year-old Bill Peascod, whose first ascent of the route had been 38 years previously.

At the foot of the crag there is a shift of tone and once the greasy rock on the early 'easier' pitches has come into play, Birkett is hoping his partner might find some reason for calling it off. By the time he has made three attempts at the crux, dithering as to whether to jam or layback it, the intonation verges on the manic. Although he had pioneered routes at a much higher standard ('New Climbs and Notes' in the same edition list a variety up to E4/5), he admitted that he had 'rarely experienced such a powerfully gripping fear'. The young man in a white sweater and stockinged feet making a nearby solo descent might have been quietly amused.

So that really was that (at least until 2014). But the climb still had one more card to play. One Saturday in June 1994, two experienced climbers, Newman and Cobbeld, were in the process of ascending the Flake. Whatever forces that had split the sliver of rock from the parent face must have decided upon a further imperceptible shift and the famous chockstone dislodged itself from the crack and fatally crushed Newman's leg. The impact on the climbing fraternity was significant. Advances in protection and footwear had all but removed the psychological element that had contributed to the difficulty of the climbs put up in the first half of the century. These were now seen as little more than interesting period pieces. The accident on the Flake put matters in a different perspective. A man can have all the friends in the world ...

Perhaps the most appropriate way to end this saga is with a twenty-first century account by an ordinary climber. Liz Cripps, a journalist, is quite happy to get to grips with the climbing walls of Shepherd's Bush and Finsbury Park in an attempt to work off the traditional excesses of her profession. She found, however, the cold and clammy hand of northern rock a rather different proposition. The piece is not only a disarmingly frank account of her own frailties but also an implicit acknowledgement of the strengths of her predecessors.

An Easy Day for a Lady?

Elizabeth Cripps, 2004

The weather teased us, as only the British weather can. Forecasts changed every half day for a week beforehand, and it was barely eighteen hours in advance that, promised a round yellow sun, we decided to make the trip to the Lakes. I rushed from London to Stockport as fast as public transport would allow (which is not fast – it took five hours) and we set off by car at 5.30 the next morning. Puddles by the roadside around Ambleside were not encouraging, but the road was dry by Cockley Beck.

We walked up Mosedale and skirted around Long Crag in early morning sunshine, watching the clouds arrange and rearrange themselves around the peaks above. Crossing the Great Moss, we could see East Buttress shiny with sunlight, only cotton wool wisps of white over its topmost pitches. Spirits rose. But not for long. Cloud loomed ahead heavy and black as we trudged up the steep haul to Mickledore (an experience for which all the treadmills in the world could not prepare me) and it started to drizzle about halfway up the scree slope. I made vague angry gestures at the sky with my walking poles, muttering darkly, and perhaps my DIY witchcraft worked, for the rain had stopped by the time we got to the coll.

Not that it was much, then, to our advantage. True, East Buttress looked bright and inviting and the light was on Scafell Pike. But Central Buttress remained wrapped in its own impenetrable white bubble. Wasdale was as invisible on one side as the Great Moss was clear on the other. The conditions were so ridiculously, frustratingly localised that they seemed invented to irritate us. Exchanging indignant remarks on the subject of weather forecasters, we abandoned packs, stamped up on to the summit of Scafell Pike (already swarming with tourists at 11.30) and returned to assess conditions.

Sliding across the stone field on the descent, we saw cloud ending in a vertical line above Mickledore, so neatly that I would have been impressed had it not exactly thwarted our plans. It would, it seemed, have been a perfect day for almost any other Lake District outing. But it was Central Buttress we had come to do, and I for one was most put out at having dragged myself up the steep slope to Mickledore, all for nothing.

The cloud cleared a moment, allowing a glimpse down into Wasdale. A glimpse, too, of the left arête of Botterill's Slab and a great deal of dark, unpromising volcanic rock. My first thought (later to be sharply revised) was that the crag didn't look as big as I had imagined. Then the mist curled itself back into place, and CB was a mystery once more.

It was 12 noon. Increasingly pessimistic but deciding to give it another hour, we opted to pass the time on Mickledore Grooves, another classic and a three-starrer to boot. The grooves, however, turned out to be a drainage gully for the East Buttress. An abundance of seepage forced HRC to abandon the attempt only about ten metres up the first pitch. By this time very disheartened (if we couldn't get up a VS, what hope for E1?) and, in my case, somewhat cross, we returned to the coll. Exactly on cue, the mist cleared. The cloud lifted completely. CB was a possibility again.

Almost ninety years earlier, Herford and Sansom climbed CB for the first time, with hemp ropes and without the benefit of modern gear. Herford, lowered down on a test run, took off his boots to climb the Flake crack. We had rock boots, harnesses, nylon ropes and a collection of wires and friends so extensive as to have added, I am sure, several kilos to HRC's weight.

Herford and Sansom's route was different, too, although the overall goal was pretty much the same – to get, by whatever means seemed most feasible, from bottom to top of the great Central Buttress. The old start was further to the left than the new one, accessed by a slippery scramble along the Rake's Progress. The first ascent avoided the top pitch, ending instead with a rightwards VS traverse. Most crucially, the loss of the chockstone in a tragic accident in 1994 turned the direct route up the crack into a dire, underprotected E3, now described as a variation. Today's climb goes out on to the Flake itself, following the line taken by Marr's variation in 1990 – a more realistic E1 5b, thanks to modern gear. There would be no call (or so I trusted) for the leader to use his second as a foothold.

We scrambled up to the Rake's Progress from the right hand side. HRC inspected the rock. 'Part wet, part dry.' We could only hope the crux pitch came into the latter category. The first two pitches, which would have been pleasant climbing in sunny conditions, were wet and unprepossessing and took much longer than they should have. Belaying at the foot of the route, wrapped in layers of fleece, I felt drips on my face and hands and hoped it wasn't raining. It was hardly more encouraging to discover that the water was descending from a large wet patch on the rock above me.

A long, leftwards-sloping ramp led to the first belay, on wires. Then a traverse left, a horribly slimy crack and an exposed walk along a ledge took us to the Oval. We had a perfect view down over Wasdale and the production line of walkers marching up to conquer the highest peak in England. But our thoughts were on what lay further up. A lake of sunshine filled the valley, reached up even to Mickledore, but the crag was firmly in the shadow, and our fingers were cold. Above us was the Great Flake and the dark, looming crack to the right of it that Herford and Sansom used such unconventional methods to defeat. But no chockstone. When HRC had done the climb a quarter of a century earlier, the chockstone had, of course, been in place. I don't know what it looked like then. Now, it looked horrible.

Cold notwithstanding, HRC set off. Reaching the bottom of the Flake without difficulty, he got a friend five in a couple of metres up the crack. It was a runner unavailable to Herford and Sansom, but he backed it up with the more traditional method of a sling around a small stone jammed in the crack above. Then our route – now the official one – departed from that taken by early ascents. HRC made the committing step out left on to a bulge on the edge of the Flake, and swung round on to the face. Progress became slow, and somewhat interesting. He completed the finger traverse left, stepped up and right to place some (very uncertain) wires, then pronounced himself baffled. The guidebook description suggests moving up right to a short slot, from which, it claims, the crest of the Flake can be 'easily reached'. But, alas, it does not explain where footholds are to be found for this simple procedure. Perhaps they are hidden underneath the moss, perhaps we went up too far to the left, but neither of us could find any.

'This is desperate,' HRC informed me – words that did little to improve the spirits of a second already cold and unaccustomed to the big mountain crags.

I could hear but not see him. I tried to think of something helpful to suggest, but failed.

'Do you want me to get out the guidebook with one hand?' I asked.

The reply was immediate and decisive: 'No. I want you to hold on to my ropes.'

Fair enough. I called back: 'I wasn't going to let go of them!' and returned to silent waiting. My hands were getting colder, and my rock boots were now so painful that I felt like the Little Mermaid, walking on knives. But Holland spent seven hours on the Oval in 1914, so I could hardly complain.

At last HRC managed to move up, taking a line further to the left than that in the description and holding on almost to nothing, hampered by rope drag and not trusting such gear as was to be had. (Later, we realised he had probably strayed on to a few metres of Foxshooter, the E4 to the left of CB.) The top of the Flake was far from 'easily reached', but somehow it was gained, after another long, tense wait. I was much relieved by the shout that heralded success – relief which lasted until he had established himself on a belay, the rope was being hauled steadily in, and I realised it was my turn.

Mabel Barker, on the first ascent by a woman, had, apparently, 'no serious difficulty with the climbing'. But my sympathy is more with Holland, who would, he said, have given up all his worldly goods, at the moment of being about to start up the Flake pitch, not to have to do it. Nor was my ascent much more dignified than his, being characterised by cowardly yells for a tight rope and frequent warnings that I was about to fall off. Moreover, while Barker, in 1925, created something of a sensation simply by being a woman, such attention as I got from the tourists below was attracted, I fear, by some very unladylike language.

I got up the leftwards-sloping crack to the Flake on tiny footholds and pulling on the edge of the crack. Without rock boots, I suppose one would have had to udge up almost inside it as best one could. By the bottom of the main Flake crack, I was extremely scared. This was a long way from the climbing walls of London. Neither the original route nor the one I was about to follow looked remotely feasible. HRC was out of sight; the outside of the Flake seemed horribly exposed and impossible, in any case, to get on to. The ground was far, far below, and my leader had just cheerfully informed me that it would be a good idea not to fall off stepping on to the Flake, because I might not be able to get back on again. And my fingertips were numb.

I complained vociferously about all these factors but, still, I got up, albeit hanging once on the rope.

The climbing, if the environment could be ignored (or appreciated) was beautifully technical – move after move for which an indoor wall can provide no substitute, and precious little preparation. A step round from overhanging crack to wildly exposed face, an intimidating finger traverse, relief as the rope ran straight above me again. Delicate steps up almost on friction, fingers clinging to the subtlest of bumps in the rock, constantly feeling that I was about to lose hold, wondering how the hell HRC had managed to keep his cool and lead this. Losing hold, regaining it, a few metres more of swearing and catching at the tiniest of edges, and finally the elation as my fingers closed round the top of the Flake. I hauled myself up with little grace but much satisfaction, and stepped cautiously along to the belay.

Not that that was the end of it. CB doesn't relent until the final metres of its 121-metre length, and we still had fifty-seven of them to go. The short pitch across and up to the start of the rightwards traverse was trivial enough. The traverse itself was less so. We had belayed below the official point, and HRC stepped up to a friend runner (no such security for the pioneers), then down, with some difficulty, on to a narrow foot ledge. A shuffle to the right, grabbing at the edge of a ledge at waist level, and then a narrow crack above gave him the chance to please a nervous second by lacing it with modern gear. After that, it was a question of negotiating a very insecure-looking spike, stepping down slightly and across on dainty holds and one crucial handhold. (Although some time was spent going too far down and climbing back up.) Then he made easy work of a corner and belayed one ledge up from the V-shaped ledge which gives the official belay.

Thanks to this thoughtfulness, I had a rope almost above me for the second half, and was rather less frightened than I had (rather vocally) anticipated. Also, the sun had crept round the top of the crag while HRC climbed, shining straight into my eyes as I perched on the belay ledge but, happily, thawing my fingers for the traverse. I had to force myself to remove the initial friend, but after that I managed the pitch rather more elegantly, and with considerably less fuss, than the previous one. Miss Barker might not exactly have been proud of me, but at least she would have been less ashamed.

The final pitch was very nice climbing – for the first half, anyway – and in very pleasant evening weather. As a Stanage one-pitcher, it would have been a beautiful VS. Some 100 metres above the ground on the Lakes' (perhaps England's) most famous route, it was just as beautiful but rather more daunting. Herford and Sansom didn't go this way, but it is hard to imagine that it could have presented any problems to climbers of their calibre. A lovely move, swinging up on a good jug and tiny footholds, then a nice, mildly technical corner crack. Then across to a corner, unfortunately very wet, but fortunately not very difficult. (The belay, however, was lovely and sunny. 'There's a beautiful view from here,' I called brightly up in the direction of HRC, but he was negotiating a waterlogged handhold and had no time for such inanities.)

From there, it was just a semi layback move with hands and feet covered in water; a ledge on to which HRC muscled and mantelshelfed and on to which I dragged myself inelegantly, face and chest first, like a seal on to a rock. Then a step up left, a couple of scramble moves, and the top. Less than thirty-six hours earlier I had been queuing for tickets amid the crowds at London St Pancras. It couldn't have seemed further away.

There are no firsts in this account to match the earlier ascents (unless perhaps this was the first ascent by father and daughter?) Nor can I do more than begin to appreciate the courage and skill of Herford et al. We had modern gear and modern guidebooks. We were climbing, not for the first time up an apparently unclimbable face, but taking the (supposedly) easiest line amid a collection of extremes. I wasn't even leading it. (I couldn't.) But for all that, CB lives up to its reputation. A climb not just worth doing, but to be proud of doing. A bloody difficult day for a lady.